Brenda

from

Brenda

John's Witness to Jesus

John's Witness to Jesus

By

JAMES L. SULLIVAN

Convention Press

NASHVILLE   TENNESSEE

Code Number: Church Study Course
This book is number 0230 in category 2, section
for Adults and Young People

Library of Congress catalog card number: 65-17037
Printed in the United States of America
425. JE 65 R.R.D.

TO VELMA

Without Mention of Her
This Book, Like My Life
Would Be Incomplete

About the Author

JAMES L. SULLIVAN, a native Mississippian, holds degrees from Mississippi College and Southern Baptist Theological Seminary, Louisville.

Twenty years a pastor, he served churches in Kentucky, Mississippi, Tennessee, and Texas. In 1953 he was called to be executive secretary-treasurer of the Sunday School Board, the Christian education and publication agency of the Southern Baptist Convention. He is responsible for administrative direction of the more than fifteen hundred employees and the twenty-five programs of work of the Sunday School Board, which serves churches in all fifty states and ninety-three foreign countries.

In addition to articles for numerous religious journals, he is the author of *Your Life and Your Church,* a book which has exceeded 1,000,000 in circulation.

Dr. Sullivan is married to Velma Scott of his own home town, Tylertown, Mississippi. They have three children: Mary Beth (Taylor), Martha Lynn (Porch), and James David, and three grandchildren.

Contents

Church Study Course

THE CHURCH STUDY COURSE began October 1, 1959. It is a merger of three courses previously promoted by the Sunday School Board—the Sunday School Training Course, the Graded Training Union Study Course, and the Church Music Training Course. On October 1, 1961, the Woman's Missionary Union principles and methods studies were added.

The course is fully graded. The system of awards provides a series of five diplomas of twenty books each for Adults or Young People, two diplomas of five books each for Intermediates, and two diplomas of five books each for Juniors.

The course is comprehensive, with books grouped into twenty categories. The purpose of the course is to help Christians to grow in knowledge and conviction, to help them to grow toward maturity in Christian character and competence for service, to encourage them to participate worthily as workers in their churches, and to develop leaders for all phases of church life and work.

The Church Study Course is promoted by the Baptist Sunday School Board, 127 Ninth Avenue, North, Nashville, Tennessee 37203, through its Sunday School, Training Union, Church Music, and Church Administration departments; by the Woman's Missionary Union, 600 North Twentieth Street, Birmingham, Alabama 35203; and by the respective departments in the states affiliated with the Southern Baptist Convention. A description of the course and the system of awards may be found in the leaflet "Trained Workmen," which may be obtained without charge from any one of these departments.

A record of all awards earned should be maintained in each church. A person should be designated by the church to keep the files. Forms for such records may be ordered from any Baptist Book Store.

Requirements for Credit in Class or Home Study

IF CREDIT IS DESIRED for the study of this book in a class or by home study, the following requirements must be met:

I. IN CLASSWORK

1. The class must meet a minimum of seven and one-half clock hours. The required time does not include assembly periods. Ten class periods of forty-five minutes each are recommended. (If laboratory or clinical work is desired in specialized or technical courses, this requirement may be met by six clock hours of classwork and three clock hours of supervised or clinical work.)

2. A class member who attends all class sessions and completes the reading of the book within a week following the last class session will not be required to do any written work for credit.

3. A class member who is absent from one or more sessions must answer the questions (pp. 146-148) on all chapters he misses. In such a case, he must turn in his paper within a week, and he must certify that he has read the book.

4. The teacher should request an award for himself. A person who teaches a book in the section for Intermediates or Juniors (any category) or conducts an approved unit of instruction for Nursery, Beginner, or Primary children will be granted an award in category 11, Special Studies, which will count as an elective on his own diploma. He should specify in his request the name of the book taught, or the unit conducted for Nursery, Beginner, or Primary children.

5. The teacher should complete the "Request for Book Awards —Class Study" (Form 150) and forward it within two weeks after the completion of the class to the Church Study Course Awards Office, 127 Ninth Avenue, North, Nashville, Tennessee 37203.

II. In Home Study

1. A person who does not attend any class session may receive credit by answering all questions for written work as indicated in the book (pp. 146-148). When a person turns in his paper on home study, he must certify that he has read the book.

2. Students may find profit in studying the text together, but individual papers are required. Carbon copies or duplicates in any form cannot be accepted.

3. Home study work papers may be graded by the pastor or a person designated by him, or they may be sent to the Church Study Course Awards Office for grading. The form entitled "Request for Book Awards—Home Study" (Form 151) must be used in requesting awards. It should be mailed to Church Study Course Awards Office, 127 Ninth Avenue, North, Nashville, Tennessee 37203.

III. Credit for This Book

This book is number 0230 in category 2, section for Adults and Young People.

Foreword

THE LIFE of Jesus on earth is recorded in four successive Gospels in the New Testament. Without conflicting, each Gospel writer presents Jesus from a different point of view. His complex nature and unique ministry as the Messiah could not otherwise be grasped adequately by the minds of men.

Matthew magnified the kingship of Jesus. Who could have done this better than the noted tax collector who so willingly turned from serving an earthly emperor to follow the King of kings? Mark stressed Jesus' deeds and sacrifice. His presentation was in the terse terms typical of such a dynamic young man. Luke dealt with Jesus as God's witness on earth, as the heavenly messenger of divine truth. These three Gospels have many similarities in their presentations of the life of Christ. For that reason they are called the Synoptic Gospels.

John's Gospel comes last and, in many ways, is supplementary to the others. Dealing with meanings more than deeds and majoring on interpretation and application, it gives significant additional insights into Jesus' life and message. This Gospel is in truth a depth presentation, revealing the nature and mission of our Lord.

The apostle states the purpose of his Gospel in John 20:31. He laments his inability to give exhaustive treatment, however, saying "that even the world itself could not contain the books that should be written" (21:25). Even so, John rejoiced that there were such inexhaustible truths to declare. There was no way in which he could completely set forth all he felt and all his heart knew. But the Gospel writer did his dedicated best, writing as the Holy Spirit inspired him and giving to the Christian world a matchless picture of Jesus Christ—God who came in the flesh.

This study course book is for guidance, designed to lead into study of the Scriptures themselves and not to be used apart from reference to the Bible. As its title implies, its emphasis is on the witness which John the beloved bore to the Master to whom that disciple had committed his all. It aims to hold up the portrait of the Lord Jesus Christ which John has painted and to lead the reader to gaze on that portrait from various angles and in various lights.

This study is not chronological. Its approach is devotional rather than expository. Little effort is made to deal with the interpretation of difficult passages. John's unique revelations of Jesus are emphasized. The organization is designed to highlight certain facets of Jesus' nature to which John bears witness. Records found also in the Synoptic Gospels are, for the most part, passed over.

Spiritual growth can best be served by a devotional rather than a critical approach in this study. The reader will wish to embark upon his search for a closer walk with Christ in prayer and self-examination. Finding the true meaning of Jesus' life lies more in a Spirit-filled heart than in a fact-filled mind. John's obvious desire was to deepen faith and broaden vision far beyond the limitations imposed by factual boundaries.

May God grant that the prayerful study of JOHN'S WITNESS TO JESUS will help the life of each learner to blossom into its fullest potential for Christian witness and service.

John's Witness to Jesus

CHAPTER 1

I. BACKGROUND
   1. Personal Testimony
   2. Authorship
   3. Circumstances
   4. Date
   5. Omissions
   6. Inclusions
   7. Characteristics

II. PROLOGUE: CHRIST THE ETERNAL (1:1–5, 9–14)
   1. Existence Before Creation (1:1–2)
   2. Activity in Creation (1:3)
   3. Visit to His Creation (1:9, 14)
   4. Rejection by His Creation (1:10–11)
   5. Acceptance by His Own (1:12–13)

1

A Gospel of Witness

John 1:1-5, 9-14

THE WRITER OF THE Fourth Gospel bears witness to Jesus as the Messiah, reveals his mission on earth, and declares that he changes human lives and eternal destinies. Clearly John states his purpose: "These [things] are written, that ye might believe that Jesus is the Christ, the Son of God; and that believing ye might have life through his name" (20:31).

I. BACKGROUND

The subject of the Gospel is Jesus. He is as much an integral part of the contents as colors in art. To show him clearly and appealingly was John's prayerful desire. With burning zeal the inspired writer presented superbly the crystal Christ in all his glory and greatness.

"Behold the man!" (19:5), a main theme in John's Gospel, may appear to contradict the marvelous way in which the evangelist magnifies the deity of our Lord. John could not adequately interpret Jesus without treatment of his humanity as well as his deity. If Jesus' mission as Messiah was to be fulfilled, he had to be fully man as well as truly God.

1. *Personal Testimony*

John wrote with the deep feeling of an intimate friend as he related what he personally knew to be true about Jesus. Thus, his Gospel is vastly more than a biography. It is a

3

witness, a testimony, a graphic portrayal by an inspired and masterful writer possessing special insights. John's loving heart made him responsive to the Holy Spirit's enlightenment and enabled him to discern deep meanings in the life and works of Jesus.

God had a special message to reveal to mankind. He waited until John's heart was ready, warmed by love, to receive and relate this message. Then the divine truths were expressed, as the Holy Spirit sharpened John's memory and guided his interpretation. (Cf. John 14:26.)

The character, influence, and ministry of Jesus, the one whom John knew so intimately, is told in vivid detail and with authoritative interpretations. John had the advantage of intimate contacts on a personal basis as one of the Lord's inner circle. No wonder men read his Gospel with such awe. Human love and divine revelation combine to portray the matchless Christ.

One of the most distinctive features of this Gospel is the emphasis on *witnessing*. Many have called attention to the prominence of this theme. The term "witness" occurs thirty-four times in verb form and thirteen times as a noun in John, a total of forty-seven occurrences as compared with only sixteen in all of the other three Gospels. The author himself does not assume the role of an instructor, as does Luke. Rather, he is a witness of the things he has seen and heard. He places himself at the side of John the Baptist and the other witnesses to the truth listed in 5:30–47. These attestations of "the witness" are not limited to the notation in 21:24 but appear throughout the book. The author is at pains to present, like an attorney, a convincing argument to the "jury," i.e., the readers, but he does more than marshall evidence and argue the case; he is also witnessing to a life he has experienced. He writes in the conviction that while it is a great privilege to be a first-hand witness, an even greater blessing is in store for those who believe on the basis of the testimony of these apostolic witnesses (20:29). As these believe they share fully in the gift of life.[1]

---

[1] George Allen Turner and Julius R. Mantley, *The Gospel of John* (Grand Rapids: William B. Eerdmans Publishing Co.), p. 3.

2. Authorship

Nowhere in the Fourth Gospel is its writer identified by name. John seems timidly to refer to himself as the author and as "the disciple whom Jesus loved" (13:23; 21:20, 24). Since earliest days, tradition has acknowledged John the apostle as the likely writer of the Gospel, the three letters which bear his name, and the Apocalypse (Revelation). Even those who question John's authorship recognize him as a resource person for many intimate items revealed throughout this Gospel.

There are many indications that the author of the Fourth Gospel was the apostle John.

Without doubt, the writer was a Jew. His manuscript shows familiarity with Jewish history and customs. He was familiar with Palestine, its people, and their worship. These characteristics fit the John whom we assume to have been the disciple who "was known unto the high priest" (18:15).

We learn from the other Gospels of John's place in the inner circle with Jesus. John observed the healing of Jairus' daughter (Mark 5:37) and the transfiguration (Mark 9:2). He participated in the Gethsemane experience (Mark 14:33). He leaned on Jesus' breast at the Last Supper (John 13:23) and raced to the tomb on the morn of the resurrection (20:3–4). Such close associations with Jesus gave John firsthand knowledge which the Holy Spirit used effectively in the apostle's revelation of his Lord.

John's background was not one of poverty, as some interpreters have suggested regarding the early disciples. His father was a man of above average means, with hired servants (Mark 1:20) and (apparently) owning his own home (John 19:27). These circumstances may have afforded John a better educational background than was usual in his day.

Salome, John's mother (Matt. 27:56; Mark 15:40), seems

to have been close to Mary, mother of Jesus, and possibly a relative. This fact could have affected Jesus' decision to commit the care of his mother into the hands of John at the crucifixion (John 19:26). Family closeness across the years would have given intimate understanding and relationships.

The Fourth Gospel shows deep emotion. This characteristic also fits John. He was anything but a calloused person. He was a bold, high-spirited man who was called "Son of Thunder" because his emotions were manifested fervently (Luke 9:49; Mark 3:17).

John is deemed to have been one of the youngest of the disciples. Thus, he could well have lived to write his Gospel many years after Jesus' ascension.

Because of internal evidence in the Gospel and the reference to "the disciple whom Jesus loved" as the one who "wrote these things" (21:20-24), A. T. Robertson and other scholars have been convinced that the writer of the Fourth Gospel was John the evangelist, later called John the apostle. With a feeling of certainty we may reach the same conclusion.

3. Circumstances

In giving his witness to Jesus, John wrote to combat certain emerging heresies. Some would-be Christian leaders had been slow to recognize the deity of Jesus. Nor were they fully convinced that he was the Messiah. John wrote to present Jesus as indeed the Son of God.

Apparently John also sought to refute certain gnostic theories which emerged during the first century—particularly the claim that Christ had not actually come in the flesh. John, therefore, magnified the humanity of Jesus even as he exalted his deity, counting as heresy the denial of either doctrine.

Another problem grew as the Christian faith extended its boundaries in the first century. Witnessing by believers swept the new religion beyond Palestine, where it had been nestled in Judaism. Many churches were predominantly Gentile in character. John recognized both Gentile and Jewish patterns of thought in his writing, as he presented the Messiah plainly and forthrightly.

The Greek language was especially suited to convey this universal witness. During the first century it was in common use throughout the Roman empire. Its extensive vocabulary made it an effective vehicle for all the New Testament writers.

4. *Date*

It is generally agreed that John's was not the first of the Gospels to be written. Mark's Gospel has that distinction, with its concise, straightforward approach to the life of Christ. Since John's writings related themselves to the heresy of gnosticism which was emerging late in the first century A.D., this approximate date seems to be suggested.

For a number of years the majority of conservative schools have held that the Gospel of John was written at Ephesus between A.D. 90 and 100—some sixty to seventy years after the crucifixion. However, recent study of the Dead Sea scrolls has caused some scholars to conclude that this Gospel must be dated earlier.

5. *Omissions*

The long list of happenings and teachings which appear in Matthew, Mark, and Luke, but which do not appear in John's Gospel is surprising. John gives no account of Jesus' birth, baptism, temptation, or transfiguration. He does not tell of the institution of the Lord's Supper, or the agonies in Gethsemane. He does not write of the ascension. He makes little reference to the parables. He omits most of the miracles mentioned in the Synoptic Gospels.

These conspicuous omissions seem to indicate that John's Gospel was written last, after he had seen the matters already discussed in the other Gospels and had deliberately decided not to repeat them as he wrote of Jesus.

6. Inclusions

Almost as surprising as the omissions in John's Gospel is the long list of things discussed by him alone. In all, only an estimated 8 per cent of John's material is duplicated in the other three Gospels. Why had not the other writers reported these things? We do not know all the answers, but we believe each wrote as he was led of the Holy Spirit, in line with the specific purpose for his Gospel.

Even where John does duplicate the record of the other Gospels, he relates details in a different way, consistent with the basic purpose of his writing. Decidedly, his is a different voice. With few exceptions, we shall confine our study to the accounts found only in John's Gospel.

John selected seven miracles to record as "signs" in line with his stated purpose. (Keep John 20:21 in mind.) Usually he follows the narration of a miracle by quoting the Master's discourse of interpretation. Some of these recorded messages are quite long.

7. Characteristics

Apparent throughout the Gospel are evidences of John's vivid memory, keen insight, and tender heart. His overflowing love was enlightened by faith's insights and by divine guidance. Through a blending of historical facts with insights which grew out of John's mature love and broad experience, the Holy Spirit used that disciple magnificently in the revelation of Jesus in his Gospel.

John's Gospel is a book of contrasts and paradoxes. It is both tender and stern, simple and complex. It magnifies such opposites as love and hate, sin and righteousness, pardon and condemnation, heaven and hell. It is a book of simple words with profound thoughts and meanings.

Mostly, John records incidents from Judea and particularly from Jerusalem. The account does not center on happenings in Galilee, as do the other Gospel writings.

John's witness is best characterized as the Gospel which depicts Jesus as Lord. It declares his oneness with the Father, his majesty and might, his creation of all things, and his universal authority. John uses indisputable evidences to show that Christ is master of the universe as well as the Saviour of the world. He makes this incomparable truth a living reality for any open mind.

Jesus' deity is magnified in many ways throughout John's record. He had glory before the earth was (17:5). He descended from heaven (6:33, 38); he knew many precise details before they were revealed to others. For example, he knew that his disciples murmured and that Judas would betray him (6:61, 64), and he knew of the death of Lazarus before men told it to him (11:14). Furthermore, (as already mentioned) his claims to deity were authenticated by his works, or "signs" (10:37–38).

Equally important is the emphasis John gave to Jesus' humanity. Though as Son of God he had shared in man's creation (1:3), he himself became man, born of woman, and he lived as a man among men. John showed how perfectly Jesus had identified himself with mankind. He was truly man as well as truly God. He was aware of man's hunger and fear (6:5, 20). He knew grief and tears (11:33, 35). He suffered thirst and cried for relief (19:28). He became tired in body and spent sleepless nights. Although, as Creator, he had caused the grain to grow, he himself endured hunger.

So complex was Jesus' human-divine nature that no man can ever fully comprehend it. Although we cannot fathom its depths, we can rejoice in the glory and wonder of this vast mystery.

Love's compulsion brought the Son of God down to earth.

The same compulsion is revealed in the statement, "I *must* [author's italics] work the works of him that sent me" (9:4).

John appeals both to the intellect and to the emotions. With a mysterious combination of simplicity and complexity, John's writings can easily get over our heads; never do they get beyond our hearts.

II. PROLOGUE: CHRIST THE ETERNAL (1:1-5, 9-14)

Matthew traced the lineage of Jesus back to Abraham and David; Luke, back to Adam. But John carried the connection back to God. From the very opening verses, his Gospel reveals Jesus as the majestic Christ, the Word who was, and is, God and who became flesh and dwelt among men.

1. *Existence Before Creation* (1:1-2)

No more meaningful statement about the person of Jesus was ever made than the declaration of his pre-existence (1:1). It is similar to God's statement about himself to Moses, "I AM THAT I AM" (Ex. 3:14), stressing the eternity of his deity. "In the beginning" gives the same context as Genesis 1:1. The words refer to time that was before the creation of the universe.

"The Word was."—Jesus was the Word, the *Logos*. Only John uses this title. A word is an outward manifestation of one's inner self and thoughts. As such, Jesus might be seen as the "divine utterance"—the outward expression of the very God.

This claim appealed to the minds of the Greeks, who stressed wisdom. They knew well and understood the meaning of *logos*—interpreted as "word" or "reason." The Jews also used this word. John chose to employ this same word, *logos*, to present Jesus as the outward expression of the character of God, the God-man who gives sense and meaning to life.

The use of the term, *logos*, implies that the order and reason which existed in the mind of God found place and meaning on earth in Jesus Christ as an expression of the mind of God. The assertion suggests control by God's mind over his universe—no matter how far it reaches into space—and over everyone and everything in it.

"The Word was with God."—Before earth was made, Christ was, and he was with God. Before the sun, moon, and stars were called into being, Christ existed with the Father. Before Bethlehem, the Son had been a spiritual being without an earthly body. In his incarnation he took on earthly form; he became man; he "emptied himself" (Phil. 2:7, ASV).

"The Word was God."—Jesus is like God, for he is God. Jesus was God's expression of himself in the flesh to men. When one sees Jesus' compassion, he can know God's concern. Jesus healed because God is burdened when men suffer. Jesus, on earth, forgave because God's heart is crushed when men err. In character and purpose, Jesus is identified with God. To know one is to know the other. Never are they in disharmony. If one misses this point, he will inadequately understand Jesus and the God he came to reveal.

Before Jesus came, many men had grossly misinterpreted the Father. They had thought God stern, unforgiving, and legalistic. Jesus revealed God as a loving Father, compassionately concerned for all mankind. Men began to see God, in the person of Jesus, wooing man to himself.

Thus, John began his witness to Jesus by declaring his eternal existence and place in the Godhead.

2. Activity in Creation (1:3)

To continue his emphasis on the preincarnation life and ministry of the Son, John declares that the Word participated in creation. "All things came into being through Him" (v. 3, NASB).[1] Man could see the hills and sky, the rivers and

---

[1] All references designated NASB are from *New American Standard Bible* (Nashville: Broadman Press, 1963). Copyrighted © by The Lockman Foundation, La Habra, California.

forests. He needed to know that these declare the eternal existence of Christ. While God the Father was the architect of the universe, God the Son was the artisan, participating in every act of creation. "All things were created by him, . . . and by him all things consist" (Col. 1:16–17).

As its creator, Christ has continuing control of the universe. He is not only the one by whom all things were made; he is the ruling Lord. In that assurance we can take comfort. God's eternal purpose of creation will be carried out, for his Son is still in charge of things.

3. *Visit to His Creation* (1:9, 14)

We can never imagine the heavenly glories Jesus Christ relinquished to come down to earth. Knowing that divine contact must be made with men if mankind was to be lifted up, Jesus stooped low to lift a fallen humanity. Man could not have his nature and course of life changed by remote control. He could not be lifted by a theory, nor by a noble ideology, but only by a Saviour, a person.

The central truth of John's witness begins to show itself in 1:14: "The Word was made flesh, and dwelt among us, (and we beheld his glory, the glory as of the only begotten of the Father,) full of grace and truth." This claim was a staggering mystery. How could the divine become human? How could spirit take on flesh? How could the Son of God become a man?

In all probability, such questions brought lengthy discussion among the Greek philosophers, who thrilled over complex intellectual challenges. Especially must John's claim have received rebuttal from the Gnostics, who felt that Jesus could not be both human and divine. But unapologetically John declared the truth of God in the flesh. He did it categorically and without compromise, declaring it an accomplished fact. God came to earth in Jesus Christ. No wonder the Son was "full of grace and truth."

4. *Rejection by His Creation* (1:10–11)

Loving darkness more than light and being given to sin more than righteousness, humankind rejected its gracious Redeemer. Men preferred their hate to his love, their darkness to his light.

Some men, no doubt, rejected Jesus because they did not understand him or the spiritual mission he had come to fulfil on earth. He was so different from their preconceived notions of the promised Messiah that they refused his call bluntly and spurned his pleas abruptly.

Other men rejected Christ because they *did* understand him and they wanted to have no part of him or his ministry. They stood at the crossroads of decision, cautiously meditating and evaluating. Deliberately they chose the road that led away from him. They did not merely neglect him; they rejected him—and with him, truth.

The fact that man can spurn his Maker reveals the kind of man God made and suggests the purpose he had in his act of creation. Man is given a will; he must exercise his choice. This freedom of the will is what makes man lovable. Otherwise, he would be a mere robot, a sort of human machine incapable of loving or being loved, of choosing or being chosen.

Jesus came to Palestine, the Land of Promise, but the populace offered little promise to Jesus. It was a land of hope to Moses and his followers, but a land of rejection for Christ. We would assume that, in the light of their background, his people would have been waiting to greet him with open arms. Their opportunities to know him had been so many. The efforts of God to reveal himself to his own had been so frequent.

Throughout their history God had sought to prepare his people for this hour when he would appear in the flesh. When the hour struck, they failed God utterly. They rejected the

Christ of prophecy. Theirs was an act of grossest tragedy, destined to bring regrets—even self-destruction.

5. *Acceptance by His Own* (1:12–13)

While many men rejected Jesus, others accepted him. The glory of faith only accents the tragedy of unbelief. "As many as received him, to them gave he power to become the sons of God."

Christ not only created the universe. His is a constant process of re-creation. The salvation of each soul is a re-creative act, divinely inspired and provided. It was to this end that Jesus came. To carry on this evangelistic and missionary purpose is the task he has given his churches on earth. Such should be the main mission of every Christian life. Bringing men to God through Christ Jesus is the task that gives life meaning and purpose.

Although men, by reason of sin, are not naturally the children of God, they do have capacity to become children of God. A sinner must become a child of God by personal encounter with faith in the Redeemer. There is no other way. Man's major victory, the conquest over sin, comes by surrender to Jesus Christ.

Thus, clearly and unmistakably, John proclaims with courageous conviction and commitment the basic Christian truths which constitute the launching pad for his book.

SUGGESTED ACTIVITIES FOR DEPTH STUDY AND ENRICHMENT

The suggestions offered at the end of each chapter include both individual and group activities. Some you may wish to carry out in class. Some may be assigned to committees for research and report. All the activities may be adapted for use by the individual learner who desires to do his own depth study. Many students will wish to record their studies in a notebook for permanent reference.

1. Turn through a harmony of the Gospels, noticing the passages found only in John. This study will concentrate on these passages. Turn through the harmony again to see the passages found in one or more of the Synoptic Gospels but omitted by John. Find as many reasons as you can why John's account is so different from that of Matthew, Mark, and Luke.

2. Find in John 20:31 the stated purpose of the Gospel writer. As you continue in this study, try to determine how each passage which you examine helps to achieve John's purpose for writing the Fourth Gospel.

3. Using a complete concordance, count the places where, in reference to Jesus, the term "Son of God" (or "the Son," with context clearly indicating "Son of God") is used. As you read the Gospel, watch for statements by or about Jesus which are equivalent to a claim that he was, and is, God the Son. You may wish to mark such statements in blue, using an inexpensive copy of the Gospel. You may wish to use another color to mark statements that show the humanity of Jesus.

4. The Gospel of John is widely used in soul-winning. As you read, mark in red those statements that would be appropriate to use to show a lost person how to be saved and what salvation includes. You may wish to ask a committee to compile a list of references to such statements for presentation to the class when chapter 3 is studied.

5. Perhaps you will agree on some committees to do the following research and report later in the study:

(1) Find and list the feasts John mentions. Using a Bible dictionary, look up such key words as: *feast, Passover, Tabernacles, Dedication.* Find out all you can about the significance of each feast and how it was observed. Bring reports from time to time as the feasts are mentioned in class discussion.

(2) Find out as much as you can about the teachings of the Gnostics. Throughout the study, call attention to ways in which John sought to refute these teachings, which apparently were taking root at the time John wrote.

CHAPTER 2

I. WITNESS IN THE FORERUNNER'S MINISTRY (1:6–36)
   1. The True Light (1:6–9)
   2. The Preferred One (1:15–16)
   3. One Greater Than Moses (1:17)
   4. The Revealer of God (1:18)
   5. One Greater Than the Heralding Voice (1:19–28)
   6. The Lamb of God (1:29, 36)
   7. The Son of God (1:30–34)
   8. One Who Would Baptize with the Holy Spirit (1:33)

II. WITNESS THROUGH THE EXPERIENCE OF THE EARLY DISCIPLES (1:35–51)
   1. Welcome for the Seeker (1:35–38a)
   2. Communication with the Learner (1:38b–39)
   3. Inspiration for the Soul-Winner (1:40–42a)
   4. Transformation for the Follower (1:42)
   5. Insights for the Open-minded (1:43–51)

III. CONSIDERED EVALUATION BY THE BAPTIST (3:22–36)
   1. Sustained Devotion (3:22–26)
   2. Recognition of Pre-eminence (3:27–28)
   3. Shared Joy (3:29–30)
   4. Acclamation of Deity (3:31–36)

IV. APPROVAL FROM THOSE WHO HAD HEARD THE BAPTIZER (10:40–42)

2

The Testimony of Many Witnesses

John 1:6–51; 3:22–36; 10:40–42

EARLY IN HIS Gospel John enriches his own strong statements about the Christ by presenting Jesus through the witness of others who knew him in his early ministry. It is significant that God has chosen human witnesses as the most effective way to make his Son known.

Many things about Jesus we do not know; the essential things we do know. His physical appearance is never revealed in the biblical account. The hue of his eyes, the color of his hair, the texture of his complexion are not noted. The size of his body is not mentioned, nor the timbre of his voice. No work of his hands remains. No page he wrote has been preserved. God thus tried to remove from man the temptation to worship a memento rather than the Master, to bow before a token and neglect the truth.

Artists reflect their own features as they seek to capture Jesus on canvas. The great Italian painters showed him with the features of a Roman. Greek artists made him Grecian. Yet Jesus "was of the house and lineage of David" (Luke 2:4), of unmistakably Jewish heritage.

In the realm of the spiritual as well as in the realm of art each person must interpret Christ in the light of his own experience, but always in accord with the revelation which the Holy Spirit gives through the Scriptures. His universality is acclaimed by the most familiar verse in John's Gospel (3:16) and by every other passage that deals with his mission to seek and save all who are lost.

17

Each man's duty is to discover and interpret Christ for himself, on bended knee with open Bible, in a questing spirit seeking divine guidance and God's revelation. Such experience lifts religion above the level of the lifeless, drab things of earth and makes Christianity sublime. It adds new dimension to life's meaning; it brings Christ near to the heart's touch and makes him real to the soul's eye.

The earlier chapters of John's book deal with the varying reactions of men as they met Jesus, what happened to their lives, and how the things they had heard about him were proven true by experience. The Gospel writer places himself alongside these other witnesses and, through them, shares with us testimony of Jesus.

I. WITNESS IN THE FORERUNNER'S MINISTRY (1:6–36)

The prologue of John's Gospel presents Jesus as one who existed before the world was, the one by whom all things were made, the divine God who had come in human form. Verses 6–36 tell of the ministry of John the Baptist. (Please read them and keep the passage open as you study this section of the chapter.) However, the primary purpose of the record is not to portray the Forerunner, but to set forth his evaluation of Jesus. In fact, the testimony of John the writer is so interwoven with that of John the Forerunner that in places we cannot be sure where one ends and the other begins. It is as if the witness of the two Johns is blended into one testimony of the Christ whom they would exalt.

1. *The True Light* (1:6–9)

John the apostle let it be known instantly that John the Baptist, great and beloved as he was, had not come to be the Deliverer, the Messiah. "He was not that Light," but came merely to bear witness to it. The record points to another as the one who "lighteth every man that cometh into the world."

God's people had experienced inner darkness. There had been no biblical prophecy since the time of Malachi, as the Old Testament was brought to a close. During four centuries prior to Jesus' coming at Bethlehem the world had experienced no great revival, no worthy reawakening, no resurgence of religious advance. Darkness—ever symbolic of death and despair, ignorance and shame—appeared to enshroud the minds and hearts and spirits of men. Into such a world Jesus came.

Ironically enough, when light did come, evil men sought to extinguish that light by murdering the Lord of life who had come to lift men out of the pit of their midnight. It seemed that they preferred their despair in darkness to the light of God's brilliant revelation.

2. *The Preferred One* (1:15–16)

John the Baptist himself repudiated the efforts of men to exalt him, asserting in his witness to Jesus: "This was he of whom I spake, He that cometh after me is preferred before me: for he was before me." Jesus Christ was, and is, the preferred one, and he alone is to be exalted. He is the one who comes to bring fulness and abounding grace to the human heart.

Verse 16 seems to be the testimony of the Gospel writer. Perhaps the Holy Spirit led him to place this statement in his manuscript as his witness to what Jesus had done for him through the years.

3. *One Greater Than Moses* (1:17)

The work of Moses is ranked lower than the work of Christ. "For the law was given by Moses, but grace and truth came by Jesus Christ." There had been a tendency in history for Moses to be placed in an elevated position. As deliverer and lawgiver, he was an ideal to the people. But Moses must be secondary to the Christ.

4. *The Revealer of God* (1:18)

Because God is spirit, men found no easy comparisons or illustrations which would interpret him to others. By sending Jesus in human flesh, God supplied the long-felt need of man for someone visible to worship. Since God has only one character, one nature, only *one* could reveal him. Jesus was that "only begotten" or unique one. So perfect is Jesus' revelation of God, that no one can understand God aright so long as he rejects God's Son.

5. *One Greater Than the Heralding Voice* (1:19-28)

Beginning with verse 19, the evaluation of Jesus is given more specifically in the direct testimony of John the Baptist. (Because of the change in the form at this point, many interpreters consider vv. 1–18 as prologue.)

In these busy days of ministry, John the Baptist was approached by traditional religious leaders of the time. They had entrenched themselves with their vested interests and stood determined to keep the status quo. When they heard of the Baptist's ministry, they were curious, and perhaps felt threatened. They could not help inquiring: Who is this man? What does he intend to do? Why does he say all this? What are his claims about himself?

It is understandable that "priests and Levites from Jerusalem" would be sent to John the Baptist to interrogate him. These men were skilled in the art of questioning. They wanted information firsthand. Possibly, they wanted also to build fences of self-protection from a rising threat they felt.

Since many people were wondering if John was the Messiah, the first question put to him by the delegation was, "Who art thou?" The Forerunner clearly declared, "I am not the Christ." In no uncertain terms he set them straight in this misunderstanding. There may have been many messianic pretenders, but the Baptist would not be one of them.

Hearing that he was not the Messiah, the investigators assumed that John the Baptist was Elijah or some other prophet from the past (Deut. 18:15). The Forerunner denied this assumption, also.

At this point John the Baptist explained his ministry to the inquiring delegation sent by the Sanhedrin (v. 23). In doing so, he revealed his own high concept of the Christ who was so important that no one else could fill his incomparable role laid out by God. It was a tremendous testimony, a thrilling interpretation of relationships.

The Forerunner was truly "the voice of one crying in the wilderness." He spoke for and of another. He was not an echo of tradition, but a vigorous voice of revelation. He heralded glad tidings. He announced to the world that a new day had dawned; a new era was on its way.

As forerunner of Jesus, John the Baptist was the preparer of the way. Obviously, men were not ready yet for the visit of the King of kings. A king's journey into an unprepared area of his dominion was preceded by a special herald sent in advance to call upon the people to prepare a highway. Volunteers would fill in the valleys, straighten out the curves, cut down the hills, and make straight a road for the king's chariot. John the Baptist came as such a herald of the King, in fulfilment of prophecy and promise. His task was calling men to remove the barriers and make passable the way for the King of kings to enter their hearts and enter their life as a nation.

The Baptist sincerely felt his unworthiness to do even the most menial tasks for the Christ. The Forerunner would have considered the privilege of untying Jesus' sandals a signal honor. Since this was a slave's task, John was saying, in essence, "The one who is coming after me is so much greater than I that I am not worthy to be his slave."

John's one function was to point men to Jesus. The Forerunner could only find failure in his own role as the announcer of Christ's coming, if men did not see Jesus in his fulness.

6. *The Lamb of God* (1:29, 36)

In rapid-fire succession, significant events are packed into the next week. The record introduces each event with "the next day" or "the day following" (vv. 29, 35, 43). Incidents seem to follow in uninterrupted sequence, but all leading to Jesus' coming.

Prophecy had predicted the race into which the Messiah would be born and the tribe and the city from which he would come. But it was John the Baptist who, in unmistakable terms, identified the individual with the words, "Behold the Lamb of God, which taketh away the sin of the world." Obviously, the reference is to the sacrifices made in Old Testament days, symbolizing atonement for sin.

The first announcement about Jesus as he launched his public ministry was the declaration of his sacrificial mission. The Passover Feast was near, and John the Baptist saw Jesus as the true Lamb of God, delivering his people. (Cf. Ex. 12:1–13.) Paul later referred to Jesus as "our passover . . . sacrificed for us" (1 Cor. 5:7). John the apostle uses the term "lamb" often in the book of Revelation. No other figure more precisely describes Jesus' costly mission to redeem a lost humanity.

7. *The Son of God* (1:30–34)

Again, the Gospel writer declared the eternity of Jesus by recording the words spoken by John the Baptist, "He was before me." (Read vv. 30–34.) Unmistakably, Jesus was identified as the Holy One, ordained by God. This identity is shown in the visit of the Spirit, "descending from heaven like a dove . . . and remaining on him" (1:32–33).

John the Baptist's mother was a kinswoman to Mary, the mother of our Lord, but it took the dove form divinely sent from above for John to know the mission of Jesus beyond any shadow of human doubt. Though he may have known Jesus intimately for years, John needed this experience to appreciate Christ's holy mission in its deepest sense.

On undisputed authority John the Baptist could declare, "This is the Son of God." His testimony was without reservation or doubt. His words show John's high concept of his holy Lord and underscore the determination of the Gospel writer to reinforce this witness.

8. *One Who Would Baptize with the Holy Spirit* (1:33)

The fact that Jesus would baptize with the Holy Spirit is expressive. "Baptize" in the Greek language means "dip" or "submerge." Thus, Jesus would saturate the souls of his followers with the Spirit of God so that they would be permeated by God's revelation and will. Baptism in, or with, the Holy Spirit would be quite different from John's water baptism, which outwardly symbolized cleansing and commitment. Under the Spirit's guidance men would know the truth, for he would be their teacher, and he would empower them to live that truth.

II. WITNESS THROUGH THE EXPERIENCE OF THE EARLY DISCIPLES (1:35–51)

The profound insights John revealed in his prologue and his account of the work of the Forerunner had come through long years of meditation, guided by the Holy Spirit. As he thought of how he and others of the early disciples had come to know Jesus, John's testimony took a different angle. He bore witness to the receptiveness and cordiality of the Lord toward those who came to him. (As you read vv. 35–51, note at least five blessings Jesus extended.)

1. *Welcome for the Seeker* (1:35–38a)

Two of the disciples of John the Baptist heard John speak,

and they followed Jesus (v. 37). The implication is that, in timidity, the disciples looked at Jesus and, in a feeling of complete unworthiness, delayed speaking until they were spoken to. Jesus' demeanor and words removed all hesitation. The seekers became relaxed in his presence. Never had they seen such greatness, such poise, such sincerity. One of these seekers was Andrew. The other is thought to have been John the evangelist, who seldom referred to himself in his writings.

Christ showed his great heart in extending a hand to encourage and inspire the timid, halting souls. He was revealing the God who in mercy will reach out to guide, if anyone will indicate the slightest interest. Knowing the inquiring hearts of the disciples, Jesus opened the conversation with, "What seek ye?" Already he knew.

2. Communication with the Learner (1:38b–39)

This initial experience of the disciples with Jesus was wonderful, but they needed more. Obviously, they wanted to linger in the presence of Jesus, so the words, "Where dwellest thou?" became natural. They wanted to fellowship with one so rare and refreshing. Perhaps they already felt in their hearts that they had found the answer to their most basic need. With overflowing souls they heard the Master invite, "Come and see."

Jesus is always glad to welcome men to personal inquiry about himself. This is the beginning of Christian life and growth.

So memorable was the transforming spiritual experience of these followers that John could point out the exact time it occurred—"that day: for it was about the tenth hour." By our clocks that would probably be about four in the afternoon, since the Jewish day began at 6:00 A.M. The new followers "abode with him that day," and their minds were never free from the impact of that momentous meeting.

3. *Inspiration for the Soul-Winner* (1:40–42a)

Fellowship with Jesus had its natural result. Andrew began his witnessing. Andrew was the kind of person who never did accomplish many notable things himself, except as he discovered others who would achieve vastly more than he himself could ever do. This ministry is illustrated in the statement, "He first findeth his own brother Simon [Peter]." Because Andrew won Peter, it is not erroneous to say that Peter's mighty words and deeds were, in a sense, those of Andrew once removed. The things Peter accomplished in life must be attributed in part to Andrew who won him to Jesus. What a wonderful way for any man to perpetuate himself and the memory of his own life.

4. *Transformation for the Follower* (1:42)

Andrew's witness brought Peter face to face with Jesus. Coming to him changes things. There is new life with a new direction and a new relationship, issuing in a new hope. Under this new loyalty to Jesus, all things are made new.

With a new love in his heart, Peter now got a new name. He had been called Simon. Did he partake of the unpredictable temper and impetuosity of the son of Jacob whose name he bore? Now he was to be called Peter, or Cephas, a rock —a name suggesting increasing steadfastness. He was to develop stability and purpose as his life grew and matured under Jesus' guidance. Although it took Peter a long time to realize the character suggested by his new name, his whole future was set in a new direction of steadfastness because he had been brought to Jesus.

5. *Insights for the Open-minded* (1:43–51)

The next ones to come to Jesus were Philip and Nathanael, whose spiritual experiences are unforgettable. Can man ever forget such a walk with God? Jesus found Philip (v.

43) and immediately Philip had to declare his experience (v. 45). That is how truth is shared. It is first met, then known.

Nathanael evidently bore prejudices toward Nazareth, the boyhood home of our Lord. At least his question, "Can there any good thing come out of Nazareth?" was sincerely asked. Philip knew that prejudices had to be removed by experience, not by argument. The best way to come to know was by a visit. "Come and see" was an invitation to Nathanael to probe personally into the truth—in the vein in which we say to others even yet, "Come, see for yourself."

Seeing, Nathanael was convinced. He declared with assurance, "Thou art the Son of God" (v. 49). At the outset Nathanael saw Jesus as both human and divine, and bore his witness in no uncertain terms.

III. CONSIDERED EVALUATION BY THE BAPTIST (3:22–36)

After a time, Jesus' public ministry brought him back into Judea, near where John the Baptist was at work. Now the Forerunner had opportunity to give his own appraisal, after he had observed the public ministry of Jesus over a period of time. The Gospel writer records the considered testimony of John the Baptist as part of the witness to Jesus.

1. *Sustained Devotion* (3:22–26)

John's loyalty to Jesus was ardent. Their ministries were parallel, and had the Baptist's heart not been right he could easily have seen Jesus as a competitor. But they mutually supported each other, as God intended. Some of John's followers did seem jealous for him, as indicated by the words: "Rabbi, he that was with thee beyond Jordan, to whom thou barest witness, behold, the same baptizeth, and all men come to him" (v. 26).

Such superimposed and unjustified sympathy can be dangerous if fed to a jealous man. Thus, men who come to feel sorry for themselves, with feeling of neglect, usually have deep resentments when such sympathy is expressed. Not so with John. He gave no evidence of envy or animosity.

2. Recognition of Pre-eminence (3:27-28)

John the Baptist stated that Jesus possessed what God had given him. The high place was, and is, rightfully his. No man can detract from him, and no man should try. John did not feel that his own disciples were being misled by Jesus, as some felt and implied. The pre-eminent place had been "given him from heaven" (v. 27), and no man could take this high position away from Jesus. God had not given the exalted place to John the Baptist; therefore, John refused to claim honor for himself at the Master's expense.

3. Shared Joy (3:29-30)

Happenings were exactly what the Baptizer had expected and what he had declared. He used an illustration of a wedding scene. Giving the figure of the bridegroom, he implied that the "best man" should not feel that the wedding discriminates against him because the bride marries the bridegroom. The best man's joy is that he has brought the bride and the bridegroom together.

The hearers surely must have caught the illustration John the Baptist was giving. Feelings of "desertion at the altar" or competition with Jesus were inappropriate and unwarranted on John's part. If one's heart is right, he will never resent any secondary role in the work of God. The Forerunner unapologetically declared, "He must increase, but I must decrease."

4. Acclamation of Deity (3:31-36)

Perhaps verses 31-36 are not the exact words of John the Baptist, but are the comment of John the Gospel writer. However, they are in accord with the attitude of John the

Baptist. He adored Jesus and happily declared, "He that cometh from above is above all." Following this testimony to the pre-eminence of Christ, there is an invitation and a challenge to men to receive the witness of the one who had come from heaven. (Read vv. 32–36.)

Jesus is presented as the one who would bring an eternal difference into the life of any man. Each man has to exercise a decisive choice, which makes him unlike other men in soul destiny. The Gospel writer saw Jesus as the one indispensable person, and he sounded a challenge something like Joshua's: "Choose you this day whom ye will serve" (Josh. 24:15).

The heart of Christian witness is the challenge to unbelievers to accept Christ as Saviour. Such witness is the responsibility of everyone who knows Jesus as Lord. And every person who receives the true witness has "set his seal to this, that God is true" (v. 33, ASV).

IV. APPROVAL FROM THOSE WHO HAD HEARD THE BAPTIZER (10:40–42)

Later in his Gospel John cites the witness of a group who had had time to make thoughtful appraisal of Jesus.

Following a move to stone him to death, Jesus withdrew to a region beyond Jordan, into the place where John at first baptized. Citizens who had known about Jesus through John the Baptist came now to see the Lord face to face. They found all that the Forerunner had said was true. John the Baptist had preached that there would be a greater one coming after him, and some hearers must have wondered how anyone could be greater than John. But here was such a one already on the scene.

Even though opposition was growing, and many fair-weather followers had turned away from Christ, we read that "many believed on him there." Such broad acceptance must have been refreshing to Jesus in the face of rising opposition.

Thus, by placing himself at the side of these other witnesses to the truth, the Gospel writer reveals how men meet the Master and are mastered by him. It is the one major relationship in which yielding brings triumph and losing oneself brings gain. Across the ages men have made this transforming discovery and in doing so have truly found themselves.

SUGGESTED ACTIVITIES FOR DEPTH STUDY

1. The chapter outline lists eight characterizations of Jesus found in the account of the ministry of the Forerunner (1:6–36). Examine each and make your own terse statement of the point made in the verses named. Recall the purpose of the Gospel writer (20:31) and decide how each of these points contributes to the aim of revealing the deity of Jesus.

2. Role playing will add meaning to this study. Imagine Andrew, John, Peter, Philip, and Nathanael seated in a group on the grass by the roadside. They are reminiscing about the time they began to follow Jesus. Be sure no imaginary details are at variance with the Scripture account.

3. A member in the role of John the Baptist may speak of his convictions about Jesus, telling of (1) first impressions, (2) deeds observed over a period of time, and (3) conclusions (3:22–36). He may borrow a well-known title and call his presentation "The Most Unforgettable Character I Ever Met."

4. As an alternate to activities 2 and 3, there may be a panel of the six characters mentioned. Each reports on "Jesus as I Saw Him in the Beginning of His Ministry." The class may ask questions of any of the speakers.

5. The class (if not too large) may become the group mentioned in John 10:41–42. They will reflect the conversation about Jesus reported by the Gospel writer. Each speaker should cite some incident to prove his observations about Jesus.

CHAPTER 3

3

Jesus' Recognition of Human Worth

John 3:1-21; 4:1-42; 8:1-11

As the Holy Spirit worked in John to guide him into all truth (16:13) and to bring to his memory what Jesus had said (14:26), the Gospel writer bore witness to Jesus' recognition of human worth. John selected a number of incidents to show Jesus' awareness of the potential for Christian character and service which was latent even in people whom others would think hopeless. Let us examine three examples.

I. Interview with Nicodemus (3:1-21)

By earthly measurements Nicodemus would stand on the top rung of life's ladder of achievement. He was in his mature years and successful in human accomplishment. As a "ruler of the Jews" he was held in high esteem. He was a Pharisee and a member of the Sanhedrin (see 7:50). As such he was responsible for teaching the religious law and interpreting it. His conduct was unquestionable.

1. *A Conscientious Inquirer* (3:1-2, 4, 9)

Nicodemus had practiced legalism personally, taught it zealously, and enforced it rigidly; yet he felt hunger in his soul. There was something deep within his heart which the law could not satisfy. Laws provided a well-ordered system, but they lacked heartbeat; they could not give life and love. Laws could give guidance, but they could not provide forgiveness for past mistakes.

31

Apparently, Nicodemus had observed Jesus. Whether his attention was claimed by the glow of the Master's mellow personality, the spark of his dynamic spirit as he cleansed the Temple (2:13–22), or his growing influence throughout the nation, we cannot be sure. Perhaps Nicodemus had heard it said that Jesus was the fulfilment of the law of Moses, writing truth in the hearts of men instead of on tablets of stone. Whatever led to the interview, Nicodemus had been impressed with what he had heard and seen.

It may be that this ruler among the Jews had honestly evaluated his own soul needs and inadequacies, existing in spite of his diligent efforts toward holy living. He earnestly desired to see Jesus and converse with him about the elements of warmth which made his life so outstanding. But could a Jewish ruler dare to approach Jesus? Criticism against Jesus began to develop early in his ministry (2:18–21), and for Nicodemus to be seen in the presence of Jesus could be the beginning of the end of his political career. Yet something drove him to take that chance.

It is unfair to criticize Nicodemus for going to Jesus by night. When the possible risks are taken into account, he should be commended for having gone at all. That is more than many men have done who have had far less at stake.

Nicodemus dared to follow the inner yearnings of his own soul. In his going to Jesus, things seemed upside down. Usually it is the young man who seeks the older, but here it was the old man who sought the younger. Ordinarily, poor men search for the rich and make requests of them. Here it was the opposite. Routinely, the schooled men are approached by those who have never been to school, in order that information may be gained. Here the man of formalized, academic training sought out the person who had never sat in a formal classroom of higher education.

The elder Nicodemus, rich and educated, sought truth and help from the youthful Jesus, who was without earthly possessions and had no place to lay his head, even when night came. Yet Jesus had much to teach. Somehow the inquirer sensed that fact deeply and sought personal conference in the late hours of darkness.

2. *The Alert Evangelist* (3:3, 5-8, 10-13)

The pent-up emotions of Nicodemus are shown by the way he began his conversation. His words poured forth like an erupting volcano. Significantly, what he was saying was true, but it was not the whole truth. Notice such designations as "a teacher," "come from God," and "no man can do these miracles that thou doest, except God be with him." Was not each statement true?

Jesus was a teacher, the Master Teacher, but that was not the main purpose of his coming. He was sent from God for a miraculous work on earth, but he was more than a heavenly ambassador. He did show his mastery over disease, demons, death, and nature. Yet, miracle-working was not the basic purpose of his ministry. If these things were all Jesus came to do, a sinner would be hopeless in his need.

Out of this background came Jesus' words: "Except a man be born again, he cannot see the kingdom of God." At first the reply seems irrelevant. Yet it did speak directly to Nicodemus' observation. In essence, Jesus was saying that, although he had done all the things Nicodemus had named, these did not constitute his main mission to earth. His basic purpose was to be the Saviour, to bring new birth to men. This was the crowning purpose of his coming; this was his mission to Nicodemus—as well as to others.

Nicodemus reacted with a revealing question, "How can these things be?" Observe that he did not ask, Why? It would seem that nowhere did Nicodemus question his *need* for salvation. He only questioned the *possibility* of it. So he asked, How?

Jesus' reply (vv. 5-6) seems to use the figure "born of

water" to refer to natural birth, as contrasted with "born of the Spirit." It is not enough to be born in the flesh. Men need to be born of the Spirit. To be born only once can be tragedy. To be born twice is glorious. It has been said many times: The man who is born only once is destined to die twice; the man who is born twice now dies but once. Here is a matter of much mystery.

Jesus went on to compare the work of the Holy Spirit to the unseen but powerful wind. Nicodemus should have been able to grasp the meaning of this figure of speech, for the Old Testament in many passages refers to the Spirit of the Lord coming upon a man in some special manifestation. But Nicodemus still asked, "How can these things be?" (v. 9).

In reply, Jesus calmly claimed to know of heavenly things through personal experience (vv. 10–13). There is no indication that Nicodemus was enraged by this claim.

3. *The Message of Salvation* (3:14–21)

Knowing that nothing else could be right until this seeker's life was made right with God, Jesus determined to clarify the doctrine of salvation, along with its importance and necessity. Patiently he went into detail with this needful man and preached one of his greatest sermons to this audience of one. That is how important one person—even one lost sinner—is in the sight of our Lord.

Since the Greek language used by John did not have quotation marks or other means of showing where direct quotation ended, we are not quite sure how much of John 3:14–21 is a verbatim report of the conversation with Nicodemus and how much may be a summary given by John. In either case we know the Holy Spirit guided John's record so that we have the heart of the truths presented to Nicodemus.

Referring to an event of Old Testament history with which Nicodemus was familiar (Num. 21:5–9), Jesus seems to say: You cannot explain how a look at the serpent of brass (or bronze) could help a sick man, but it did. When the people accepted the plan given them by God, they received physical healing. Even so, "the Son of man" must be "lifted up," and trust in him will bring spiritual life to those who accept God's plan.

One wonders if it was only when Nicodemus saw Jesus on the cross that he understood these words, and seeing Jesus "lifted up," acknowledged his right to claim the messianic term, "the Son of man."

In this connection we are given one of the most glorious texts of the Scriptures, John 3:16. God is shown as the greatest giver; Jesus is declared as the greatest gift; and salvation is proclaimed as the greatest guarantee. Divine love is magnified. God loves because it is God's nature to love. Therefore, it is not his desire to destroy unworthy men, but to remake them through a spiritual rebirth.

Nicodemus walked away from the interview apparently impressed. But he departed without open commitment, as far as we can tell. Maybe he counted the cost and reckoned the risks too great. Did he, in his own mind, see the possible loss of position, the confiscation of his property, and even the loss of his life? Jesus could give much, but would it be worth such a cost to Nicodemus?

Deliberating these matters of soul need and God's redeeming grace and mercy, Nicodemus went away silently. At the same time, we must assume that something significant had happened within him. Indications are that he thought he could be a secret disciple.

As Jesus' ministry advanced, the storm clouds darkened around him. Finally, the fury of human animosity swept him to Calvary's cross. In that unequaled moment there were two courageous men who dared to show themselves friends of the crucified one. They dared to request his body that they might lay it away. Those two men were Nicodemus and

Joseph of Arimathea, who owned the grave (19:38–42).

In light of the last recorded acts of Nicodemus, it seems logical to believe that he had caught the truth of Jesus' words and, having reached his conclusion, braved the opposition to declare publicly his belief in Jesus as the Christ. He had seen in the Master a new purpose and new possibilities for his life. Nicodemus was willing to face the future with the reward of these new dimensions, regardless of the personal sacrifices involved.

Through recording the interview with Nicodemus, John bears witness that no life, whether high or low, is adequate apart from Christ. He sees the worth in every life and the unrealized victories in every man. The touch that only Christ can give brings men to realize their greatest potential. An introduction to him is something all men need.

II. INTERVIEW WITH THE WOMAN AT THE WELL (4:1–42)

Closely following the record of Jesus' nighttime discussion with the noble Nicodemus, the Gospel writer gives us the story of the interview with the unworthy woman at the well of Sychar. The sequence in John's Gospel is significant. Ministry to the higher-ups in human achievement and ministry to those less fortunate, even the fallen, came within the scope of Jesus' concern and assistance.

The woman of Samaria was not only a sinner, but a foreigner. Barriers were high, yet Jesus rolled all of them back. Needs were great, but Jesus met them with his divine power and without reluctance. (You will do well to read the entire story from your favorite translation.)

1. *Awareness of Opportunities* (4:1–7)

It is easy for one preoccupied in duty and exhausted in travel to seek rest for his own weary body and to excuse himself from the Christian obligation of witnessing. Jesus, our example, never yielded to such a temptation. His sense

STOP.

of spiritual obligation never dwindled; his care for human need never wavered.

With his disciples Jesus was traveling through Samaria. That fact in itself was remarkable. The strictest Jews traveled from Jerusalem by crossing over the Jordan, going northward to a point near the Sea of Galilee, and then entering Galilee at a place which would avoid Samaria altogether. But to Jesus the Samaritans were people, and they needed his help. He would not avoid or neglect them.

Wearied in his travel, Jesus slumped in bodily exhaustion at Jacob's well, while his disciples went into the nearby village to buy bread for the travel party.

At an odd hour for one to draw water, the woman of Samaria came to the well. Jesus at once sensed her inmost spiritual needs. Not only was she of an unfortunate race, but she seemed not to be accepted even among her own misfit people. Did she come to draw water at noon to avoid crowds at the regular time in the late evening? Perhaps so. If this is true, it could indicate that she was either a "loner" or an outcast. Her future seemed no more promising than her past, until she met Jesus.

Forgetting his tired body, Jesus devoted himself to one thing, the meeting of the soul needs of this unworthy woman. She belonged to a people who were the product of unfortunate mixed marriages at the time of the Assyrian conquest of Palestine. Being a mixture, the Samaritans were not acceptable to either of the diverse races. Added to this problem was the woman's own lax morality. Apparently, she was willing to take up with different men at different times without bothering about marriage vows. Her spiritual needs were intense. Her heartache was great. What could Jesus do?

Jesus tackled the problem head-on and dealt with the woman's need in all of its ramifications. He not only wrought a miraculous change in her heart and life, but in doing so he gave his followers some specific helps in personal evangelism. His act revealed that no one is worthless, no person lacks potential for good, and no one is beyond hope.

2. *Lessons in Soul-Winning* (4:7, 9–26)

Jesus' techniques in bringing about the transformation in this woman's life are revealing and inspiring.

He was burdened for one who apparently lacked concern for herself. He dared speak to her, although he knew that such conversation was taboo in the eyes of Jews and Samaritans alike. Perhaps he anticipated the tongue lashing he received from her in the words, "The Jews have no dealings with the Samaritans" (v. 9).

He began at the point of her own conscious need, deep thirst. He talked of water, the very thing she had come to get. He spoke a plain language she understood and communicated profound theological truths to her mind, which had no theological background.

The woman was apparently amazed that this strange man showed an interest in her spiritual welfare or that he even cared. Compassion truly counts. Without it, knowledge and vision falter. Jesus dealt delicately with the woman's sins. He told her about her careless past in such a way that he did not repel her, but rather led her to seek more guidance and to yearn for cleansing.

He led her to think of the Messiah, and identified himself as that one who would meet her spiritual thirst with living water. He wanted her to know that lives must be lifted by the personal Saviour, not by coercion or legislation. He revealed the fact that her soul needs could be met by the Redeemer, who would change every area of her life.

3. *Witness of a Believer* (4:28–29, 39–42)

Evangelism's purpose is best expressed when those who are evangelized become, in turn, evangelists. When the woman at the well heard Jesus' revelation of himself, she trusted. Then she hastened to let others know the inner joys her heart had come to know. She rushed into the nearby city crying, "Come, see a man" (v. 29). As a result of her witness, "many of the Samaritans of that city believed" (v. 39), not simply because they heard her testimony and observed the tremendous alteration in her own life, but because, at her invitation, they had come themselves to see and to hear Jesus. They went away knowing that "this is indeed the Christ, the Saviour of the world" (v. 42). We wonder whether the disciples, when they went into the city, had been as eager as was this woman to bear witness regarding the Christ.

4. Happiness in Ministry to Human Need (4:32–34)

The happiness of the woman—who was so overwhelmed that she forgot her errand and went away leaving her water-pot at the well—is only half the story. Jesus had been hungry and tired when, in the heat of the day, he arrived at the well in Sychar. Soon he forgot both hunger and fatigue. Concerned with the woman's salvation, he overlooked his own exhaustion and launched into an aggressive evangelistic effort with the freshness and alertness of an early morning. When his disciples returned with the bread they had bought, Jesus explained his resurgence of energy and vigor by saying, "I have meat to eat that ye know not of" (v. 32). Great was his joy.

5. A Pattern for Jesus' Followers (4:35–38)

In Jesus' approach and words, he provided his followers with guiding principles for all time in their evangelistic efforts. Such words as, "God is spirit; and those who worship Him must worship in spirit and truth" (v. 24, NASB), suggest that in soul-winning as in worship it is not the place but the attitude that counts most. Souls can be won as readily at a well curb as at an altar, for God is everywhere.

Jesus challenges all disciples: "Behold, I say unto you, Lift up your eyes, and look on the fields; for they are white already to harvest" (v. 35). Thus he constantly magnifies the emergency of the task of evangelism and the immediacy of the responsibility of all believers to give guidance to others who need to know the way. The one who has been saved has a story to tell and must proclaim it anywhere and to any person.

Through his record of the woman of Samaria, John bears witness to Jesus' estimate of the worth of those whom the world considers worthless, unfortunate, downcast. He also bears witness to another truth: the follower of Jesus cannot permit himself to be sidetracked from his main duty or to ask exemption from Christian responsibility.

Jesus sees people not only for what they are, but views them in the light of his redeeming love and transforming grace. Jesus does change lives. In redeeming them he alters everything about them for all eternity.

III. Woman Taken in the Act of Sin (8:1-11)

Jesus' concern for unworthy, even outcast, people is further revealed in the account of the woman caught in adultery.

The earliest Greek manuscripts do not record John 7:53 to 8:11 as a part of the Fourth Gospel, although it is reasonably well established that the verses tell of an actual incident in the life of Jesus. You will notice that in many translations these verses are set off in some distinctive place or type, with a note of explanation. However, the account in 8:1-11 excellently sets forth Jesus' indignation toward hypocrisy and his patience with an unworthy humanity. Therefore we have chosen to deal with it.

We need to understand what is being said to us about Jesus through this occurrence. His tenderness in dealing with this unworthy soul is contrasted with the sternness he showed toward self-righteous critics who sought to exalt themselves by degrading others.

1. *Efforts to Embarrass Jesus* (8:4-6)

The scribes and Pharisees were hostile toward Jesus. In every way possible they sought to trap him with perplexing questions, wanting somehow to trick him into conflicting statements or to thrust him into a dilemma. In "tempting him" (v. 6) they had ulterior motives, but Jesus understood their scheme and was equal to the situation. He knew the human tendency to pass judgment on others, and he knew that no man was capable or worthy of doing so. In fact, the disposition of the man with the greatest flaws is to focus on flaws in others. The harshness of these accusers was brutal, if not vulgar. They so majored on the woman's wrong that they had no time to consider their own.

Confronting Jesus with the undoubtedly open guilt in this sunken life, these smug sinners sought his judgment and condemnation of her. Their purpose was to show that his preaching of mercy was a farce. If he did not condemn the woman, they could accuse him of treating sin too lightly. In that way they could set him in conflict with Moses' law. If he did condemn, they would want him to order her death. Jesus would not be so snared. With insight he made a clear distinction. Sins are to be condemned; sinners are to be forgiven when they repent.

2. *Challenge and Warning* (8:7-9)

At this time Jesus wrote, as far as we know, his only words, and they were sketched in sand. They were for effect more than for permanent record. The deliberate plot to discredit Jesus centered on Moses' law (Lev. 20:10) which was quite clear-cut regarding adultery. The woman in this case was only incidental to the base purpose of these vicious men. They were after Jesus, and she was being used for their purposes.

Jesus surprised the accusers by permitting their consciences to be pierced by their own attack. Shocked into silence by the unexpected turn of events, they stealthily slipped away one at a time. Only Jesus stood guiltless. He would show pity instead of cruelty. The delicacy with which he dealt with the woman reveals his own nobility. He sought restoration instead of condemnation. That the same spirit should characterize his followers is an inescapable deduction.

3. *Hatred for Sin, Love for Sinners* (8:10-11)

Jesus' love showed through. He did not question the woman's guilt, so he did not acquit her. Instead, he turned to indict the accusers for their own sins. He had pity toward the one who had made a serious mistake. But he revealed sternness toward spiritually disfigured men who claimed to be righteous and publicly paraded a make-believe self-righteousness. The soul disease of the sinner was loathsome, but the Great Physician's ministry was one of healing. He had not come to condemn but to make whole.

This was more than just a test case. Over a period of years, no woman had been stoned to death for adultery, even though the Mosaic law ordered it. Jesus used the occasion to show that a fallen woman is degraded by man's lust and that in spirit the accusers are often as guilty as the accused. Jesus did not condemn her, nor did he justify her, but he did call her henceforth to a life of chastity.

Once again, this remarkable incident demonstrated Jesus' love for souls and his determination that lives shall be lifted by his healing power.

SUGGESTED ACTIVITIES FOR DEPTH STUDY

1. Compare the accounts of Jesus' dealing with Nicodemus, the Samaritan woman, and the woman taken in adultery in respect to: (1) the personal need of the individual in each case;

(2) evidences of Jesus' estimate of human worth; (3) how the message of salvation was presented to each; (4) how each person was changed.

2. Consider other ways the Gospel of John states the experiences of salvation. If a committee has been making this study, they may check their list of references against the following before they report. They may wish to add other passages and to share the entire list with the whole class: 1:12–13, 29, 36; 3:3, 5, 14–15, 16–18, 36; 4:10, 14; 5:24; 6:29, 33, 35, 37, 40, 47, 51, 53–58; 7:37–39; 8:12, 24, 31–32, 36; 9:5, 35; 10:9, 11, 27–30; 11:25–26; 12:25–26, 36, 44–47; 13:20; 14:12, 15, 21, 23; 17:3, 8, 21–23; 20:30–31.

In reporting, the committee should read some of the most significant passages and indicate what aspect of salvation each sets forth. Consider, in each case, how this aspect of salvation is further evidence of the potential worth of an individual in God's sight.

From the list of passages presented, each class member may select those he would like to mark for easy reference in his soul-winning efforts. Many soul-winners like to carry a small, paperbound Gospel of John in which they have underlined in color verses that relate to salvation.

CHAPTER 4

I. Turning Water into Wine (2:1–11)
    1. Gala Occasion (2:1–2)
    2. Pending Humiliation (2:3–5)
    3. Miraculous Demonstration (2:6–11)

II. Healing the Nobleman's Son (4:46–54)
    1. Physical Need (4:46–47)
    2. Heart Heaviness (4:48–49)
    3. Divine Healing (4:50–54)

III. Healing the Lame Man (5:1–16)
    1. The Miracle (5:1–9)
    2. The Sequel (5:10–16)

IV. Feeding Five Thousand (6:1–14)
    1. The Dilemma (6:5–7)
    2. The Scant Resources (6:8–9)
    3. The Adequate Christ (6:10–14)

V. Walking on the Sea (6:15–21)

VI. Healing the Man Born Blind (Chap. 9)
    1. Act of Healing (9:1–12)
    2. Agitations Because of the Healing (9:13–23)
    3. Testimony of the Healed (9:24–34)
    4. Identification of the Healer (9:35–41)

VII. Raising Lazarus from the Grave (11:1–54)
    1. Love's Purposeful Delay (11:1–16)
    2. Sincere Sympathy (11:17–38)
    3. Lord of Life and Death (11:39–45)
    4. Organized Opposition (11:46–54)

4

Witness Through Miracles

John 2:1–11; 4:46–54; 5:1–16; 6:1–21; 9:1–41; 11:1–54

WE THINK OF AUDIO-VISUAL methods of teaching as a recent development. Appealing to the eye as well as the ear in instruction, however, is a historic and proven technique. Jesus used it. Though he did not have motion pictures, filmstrips, flip charts, and many other teaching aids, his miracles were audio-visual instruction at its best.

John selected seven miracles, or signs, to record as his witness that Jesus was the Son of God. In most instances John records the miracle and then a discourse based on the miracle. However, at this point in our study we shall focus on the event and, in several cases, leave the discourse to be treated in another setting. As we consider each miracle we shall seek to determine what was the characteristic or special ministry of Jesus that John was emphasizing as he made the record.

I. TURNING WATER INTO WINE (2:1–11)

Jesus' first miracle occurred not at a religious gathering in Jerusalem, but at a social event in Galilee. Yet, through this event, those closest to Jesus could glimpse what it meant to walk with the Son of God (v. 11).

1. *Gala Occasion* (2:1–2)

According to custom, much ado accompanied this wedding feast. Apparently, a large crowd was present, including Jesus and his disciples. The bride and groom, no doubt at-

45

tired in appropriate robes, were treated like royalty. Serving wine at such an occasion was the traditionally accepted procedure. In the arid East, thirst was parching, and available water was often unpalatable. Serving wine was an expression of hospitality to weary travelers, many of whom came from afar.

2. *Pending Humiliation* (2:3–5)

Since Cana is not far from Nazareth, it was natural that Mary, the mother of Jesus, would attend the wedding feast. Evidently she considered herself a sort of cohostess, and she was bothered no little at the likelihood of running out of wine. The festivities usually lasted much longer than a day, and lack of refreshments could create a serious problem. The embarrassment also could leave bitter memories for the wedding couple. In this situation Mary reported the problem to Jesus.

Jesus' words, "Woman, what have I to do with thee?" when said in English seem disrespectful and blunt. That was not true in the original language. "Woman" was the term of endearment (19:26), and the expression, "What have I to do with thee?" shows no disrespect or rebuke. It suggests that there were aspects of this which were not clear to her at the time and that everything should be left to Jesus. In perfect confidence Mary gave orders to the servants to do whatever Jesus told them.

3. *Miraculous Demonstration* (2:6–11)

Drawing water according to Jesus' instructions, the servants filled the six water jars. These containers, holding twenty to thirty gallons each, were used to hold water for the numerous ceremonial cleansings practiced by the Jews.

It is not clear from the record whether the one hundred twenty gallons of water were turned to wine or whether the water was turned to wine as it was drawn. If the latter was the plan, then Jesus supplied just what was needed, as it was needed.

When the wine had been drawn from the waterpots, the headwaiter, or "governor of the feast," was given the first taste. Astonished, he commented that the bridegroom had kept the best for the last.

John tells us that through "this beginning of miracles . . . in Cana of Galilee," Jesus "manifested forth his glory; and his disciples believed on him." To these men who had left all to follow Jesus, there must have been reassurance in the realization that he could and did supply the need which was referred to him. Most of the miracles reported in the Gospels show Jesus meeting desperate need. In this, the first recorded miracle, his loving concern seems especially tender because it is exercised just to prevent embarrassment and to increase the joy of a social occasion. Its purpose was to interpret and exalt Jesus as one with concern and power, one who was divine but available to man.

II. HEALING THE NOBLEMAN'S SON (4:46–54)

In this same Cana another miracle was performed. This second sign served to reveal Jesus' power over disease and distance and to increase men's knowledge of who Jesus was and what he had come to do, as well as to interpret his compassionate concern for people with heavy hearts.

1. *Physical Need* (4:46–47)

From Capernaum a nobleman traveled some twenty miles to seek assistance from Jesus. This royal officer may have been a man of fortune and authority, but he felt utterly helpless when his son became critically ill. In desperation he turned to Jesus, praying for help. Jesus gave it gladly.

It took real faith on the nobleman's part to believe that a carpenter from nearby Nazareth could possess healing power. So many men and women who lived close to Jesus never understood why he came. They saw the sweat of Jesus' brow and the callouses of his hands as he worked in the carpenter's shop. but they never saw the remarkable truth that he was the Son of the Almighty God. Proximity seemed to produce blindness for them. For the nobleman, an urgent need had helped to overcome his pride and to open his eyes to the one who could render assistance.

2. *Heart Heaviness* (4:48–49)

Jesus' first words in this situation were spoken for the sake of the observers as well as to test the sincerity of the nobleman. The sensation hunters must have watched intently to see the results. If the man's coming had been lacking in sincerity, he might have been irked at Jesus' words, "Except ye see signs and wonders, ye will not believe."

But the father did not despair. His need was too great. His frantic appeal for help revealed his tremendous love for his child. He was begging for Jesus' sympathy and assistance, and he would allow nothing to deter him. His simple faith is proved by his words, "Sir, come down ere my child die." Seeing the man's trust and perseverance, Jesus was ready to act.

3. *Divine Healing* (4:50–54)

The unexpected happened. Instead of accompanying the father to the home, as a physician usually would, Jesus, separated from the patient by about twenty miles, pronounced the son well and sent the father on his way. When the father turned his face from Jesus and started homeward, he had no outward evidence that his prayer was answered. But he did have Jesus' word of assurance. That was sufficient.

While en route home, the father received news of his son's healing. Recovery could be pinpointed to the moment Jesus spoke the words indicating that the son was healed. Rewarded faith now resulted in unlimited love. The father and his whole household had a new Master. Beginning with a sense of need, the happy incident ended with a redeemed household launching into its future as one of the first truly Christian homes.

This was the second sign, or miracle, that Jesus did in Cana. The first had shown his power over nature; this one his power over disease. The miracle also demonstrated a principle that is evident in each healing miracle John records: Believing comes before seeing; obeying precedes the experience of the blessing; as men act on the command of the Lord, they open the way for his power to operate in their lives. Emphatically Jesus had again revealed his deity by his miraculous act. Anguished hearts find balm in Christ.

III. HEALING THE LAME MAN (5:1–16)

Who could have been more lonely or helpless than the invalid who had not walked in thirty-eight years and who had failed to find one friend who would try to help him? In dealing with the man, Jesus wanted to show that human need was more important than religious legalism and to reveal himself as the healer with a heart of concern.

1. *The Miracle* (5:1–9)

Three major feasts were named in the Old Testament (Deut. 16:16). Every adult male (unless incapacitated) was commanded to attend. We may be sure that Jesus came because he counted it joy to be with the people he loved.

It was during one of these well-attended feasts that Jesus healed the lame man at Bethzatha (Bethesda), a famous and historic pool. The waters of underground streams periodically gushed forth into the pool. Tradition attributed the unusual occurrence to an angel and held that the first one who entered the waters after the turbulence would be healed of his affliction. The lame man had never been told any other way to be cured. (Actually, verse 4 does not appear in the oldest manuscripts. It is omitted in ASV and RSV.)

Jesus was sympathetic with the lame man's plight and desires. Rather than reprimand him for trusting the healing waters, Jesus ignored the tradition and challenged the man with the order, "Rise, take up thy bed, and walk." As the man obeyed, he was healed. He not only arose and walked, he took with him the mattress used for a bed. What an evidence of the healing power of the Christ who cares!

2. *The Sequel* (5:10–16)

It was the sabbath when the healed man performed the "work" of lifting his bed, thereby violating the stringent sabbath laws of the Jews. On being attacked for sabbath violation, the one healed replied that the healer had ordered him to take up his mattress and walk. Not knowing the identity of the healer, the man cured was, nevertheless, ready to accept the appropriateness of his instruction. Surely one who could work such a miracle must know right from wrong. Later, Jesus found the man in the Temple. Revealing his interest in the man's soul as well as in his body, Jesus instructed him, "Sin no more."

When the restored one identified his benefactor, the critics cruelly turned on Jesus. John's record of this miracle is a witness to Jesus' power over long-term impotency, over sin in a life, and over legalism which would leave a man in his helpless state. In a later chapter we will discuss John's record of how Jesus turned this problem situation into a teaching opportunity.

As he revealed the worth of even a crippled man, Jesus proved also his own divine power which makes men spiritually whole.

IV. FEEDING FIVE THOUSAND (6:1–14)

Although this miracle is presented in the Synoptic Gospels, it needs discussion here also because of the additional truths John records—for example, the presence of the lad with the loaves and fish, the problem posed to Philip, and Andrew's part in finding the lad. These details of human action are in the record which emphasizes Jesus, the Son of God.

1. *The Dilemma* (6:5–7)

Jesus with his disciples crossed Galilee to enjoy some restful hours, but the multitudes continued to follow in huge numbers. Walking around the Sea of Galilee to the north and fording the upper Jordan, they came to the point on the far side of the sea where Jesus and his disciples had arrived.

Seeing the multitudes, Jesus put a question like this to Philip, "How are we to buy enough food for all these people?" Philip's estimate meant the equivalent of two thirds of a laboring man's wages for an entire year in order to provide even a bit of food for each person present.

2. *The Scant Resources* (6:8–9)

Into this crisis of hunger moved Andrew—one of the most neglected men of the Scriptures. Somehow he had discovered a lad who had loaves and fishes. The lad was led to Jesus with the suggestion of the food's availability in feeding the multitude. After making the suggestion, however, Andrew timidly backed away with an apologetic question, "But what are they among so many?"

2. *The Adequate Christ* (6:10–14)

Jesus, as always, was adequate to the situation. He received what the lad offered, gave directions for organizing the group, and increased the few loaves and fishes into a supply sufficient to feed the five thousand. Miraculously, he broke bread bit by bit and produced enough to supply each person food in abundance. After the multitude had been fully fed, there were twelve baskets remaining, showing the superabundance of the supply.

Even the lad who had voluntarily surrendered his all to

Jesus now had available more food by far than he had yielded, but along with the others he no longer hungered. The lad learned that there is no such thing as permanent sacrifice when one follows Jesus. One gets back more than he gives.

This miracle shows Jesus' concern for human need and his power to meet it. It shows how much Jesus can do with so little. Moreover, it reveals his need of human channels through whom to pass his blessing to the needy multitude. Seeing the miracle, the observers recognized him as "that prophet that should come into the world" (v. 14).

V. WALKING ON THE SEA (6:15-21)

The miracle of walking on the water is also recorded in Matthew 14 and Mark 6. We include it in this study because of its significance in John's purpose for his book.

The Sea of Galilee is as treacherous as it is beautiful. Danger comes when unpredicted air currents move down quickly from the mountains. Like the notorious "blue northers" in the Southwest, this freakish, sudden shift of air causes an instantaneous downdraft. It can churn the waters of the sea furiously. The disciples, recognizing the danger, were uneasy when they were caught in such a storm in the darkness of midnight.

Jesus had a special eye for human need, whatever it was. In spite of his own deep need, which had sent him alone to a mountain for prayer (v. 15), he was aware of the plight of his own disciples, who were nearest to him. Walking toward them, he calmed his distressed followers with the words, "It is I; be not afraid." Persuaded that he was not an apparition, they willingly received him into the boat. Instantly, the boat was at the shore—at their precise destination.

This miracle emphasizes the control of the Creator over the elements and over human fear. In life's tense, terrifying situations, which are inevitable, it is comforting to know of one who does care and who is able to aid a helpless, fearful humanity. Such is the witness to Jesus in John's record of this miracle.

VI. Healing the Man Born Blind (Chap. 9)

Life in Palestine was hard at best. Hard work and late hours were required of a healthy man to meet life's demands. Imagine the plight of a blind man—especially one who had been born blind. In recording the healing of such a one, John reveals Jesus' compassion and his authority.

1. *Act of Healing* (9:1–12)

Enemies of Jesus had gathered stones to kill him, "but Jesus hid himself, and went out of the temple, going through the midst of them, and so passed by. And as Jesus passed by, he saw a man which was blind from his birth" (8:59 to 9:1). How tender the heart of one who, under such trying circumstances, could see a poor blind man and pause to heal him.

Across the ages some misguided men have tried to relate human suffering to some specific human sin. The disciples were caught up in such a traditional inference and inquired of Jesus who it was who had sinned, whether it was the victim or his parents. Thoughtlessness in such a question is obvious. How could an unborn child sin?

Jesus taught that acute hardships do not necessarily have direct relationships to specific human transgression. Here the affliction was allowed for the purpose of divine glory (v. 3). Anointing the eyes of the man, Jesus commanded him to wash with water at a specific place. Doing so, he was cured. The healed blind man helped give indisputable evidence that Jesus is divine.

2. *Agitations Because of the Healing* (9:13–23)

Sometimes healing poses problems as great as those of

affliction. In this case, restoration produced a vigorous argument. Critics contended that Jesus could not be divine and gave as their reason that he healed on the sabbath. Others answered in defense that he could not have healed had he not been from God. So an argument raged. Some skeptics scoffed that the blind man really had never been blind at all and that the whole incident was a hoax.

The parents of the restored man gave witness only that he was their son and that he had never been able to see at all. They sidestepped the issue when they heard threats of exclusion from the synagogue for anyone who might indicate that Jesus was the Messiah (v. 22). Questioners were referred to the son. Being of age, he could give his own testimony.

3. *Testimony of the Healed* (9:24–34)

The critics tried to put words into the mouth of the healed man by suggesting that he should give all the glory to God the Father. They suggested that none should be given to Jesus, for said they, "This man is a sinner." But the healed man would not be misled, nor would he be silenced. In clear-cut terms he testified, "One thing I know, that, whereas I was blind, now I see." He accused his interrogators of shutting their own eyes to absolute evidence, their ears to truth, and their hearts to faith. With physical eyes open, they were blind with wilful sightlessness.

Risking the consequences from the biased critics of Jesus, the man affirmed, "If this man were not of God, he could do nothing." Not being able to answer such logic and testimony, they excluded the man from the synagogue (v. 34). They would henceforth ignore him. In their minds they had left no place for light.

4. *Identification of the Healer* (9:35–41)

Puzzled by the things he had experienced without comprehending, the healed man yearned for more understanding. Jesus took the initiative and found the man. The healer identified himself as the Son of God and stated, "Thou hast both seen him, and it is he that talketh with thee."

The hungry heart had found its answer. Faith expressed itself verbally, "Lord, I believe." The onetime blind man worshiped the newfound Lord who had given him life as well as light. His healing had progressed from physical sight to spiritual insight.

There is a progression in the miracles of healing which John selected to include in his witness—a sick child, a chronic invalid, and a man born blind. Each miracle deepens the witness to the compassion, power, and authority of Jesus.

VII. RAISING LAZARUS FROM THE GRAVE (11:1–54)

All four Gospels refer to the power of Jesus over death. Only John tells of the raising of Lazarus, who had been dead so long that it was natural for his sister to assume that by that time decomposition had already begun.

1. *Love's Purposeful Delay* (11:1–16)

Mary and Martha, residents of the village of Bethany, became grievously concerned when their brother's illness became severe. Their first thought was to get the word to Jesus, their best friend. He would not only care, he would know what to do. They must have been startled to learn that Jesus deliberately delayed coming to their side in this extreme emergency.

Jesus lingered, not because he did not care, but because he did. He was willing for loved ones to suffer anxious moments temporarily because, out of his later arrival, they would receive glorious revelations of himself not available otherwise. He must time his works by his own wisdom and not by man's. Therefore, Jesus tarried for two days, apparently for the purpose of letting death occur. Friends of Jesus needed to learn that the Lord of life is victor over death.

Returning to Bethany held its hazards just then, and Jesus placed his own life in jeopardy to bring life to another. He knew Lazarus was dead, though he used a customary word, calling it "sleep" (v. 11). Thomas took a dim view of things, thinking Jesus was leading them into the portals of death instead of the arena of eternal life. But Thomas remained loyal.

2. *Sincere Sympathy* (11:17–38)

In the presence of many friends, Jesus consoled Martha and, later, Mary. Their grief had led them to a distraught state of mind in which they were apparently censuring the Lord for not having arrived on time. When Jesus spoke to Martha of the raising of Lazarus, her natural conclusion was that he must have been referring to the "resurrection at the last day," but he was not.

Heavy of heart, and sensing the sorrow of the bereaved sisters, Jesus wept *with* them, not just *for* them. Tears were briefly shed, then the power of Jesus' presence began to flow in fullest measure.

3. *Lord of Life and Death* (11:39–45)

Jesus commanded that the stone be rolled away from the tomb. In prayerful posture, he talked to God. Then he commanded the grave to yield its dead. Death had met its master; the tomb had met its conqueror. Lazarus came forth, and the graveclothes were loosened—his return to life proof of the power of the Lord of life.

So indisputable was Jesus' authority over death that many believed. Jesus' purpose in performing the miracle was completed. It was a sign of his deity and many accepted this evidence, for "many . . . believed on him" (v. 45).

Kyle M. Yates, in his book *Preaching from John's Gospel,* (p. 109) appropriately says:

This incident gives these distinct lessons: (1) Love permits pain and sorrow and heartache that individuals may be driven to the Christ and that his love and sympathy and power may be made manifest. (2) Love leaves prayer unanswered or postponed. (3) Love comes at length with blessings which are indescribably and immeasurably glorious to make certain that glory comes to the Father. It is Christ's way of dealing with his needy ones.

4. *Organized Opposition* (11:46–54)

Already there had been indications of combined animosities. Following the raising of Lazarus, Jesus' enemies engaged in co-ordinated action. "The high priests and the Pharisees called a meeting of the council" (v. 47, Williams).[1] The high priest then and there predicted Jesus' death (v. 51). The plot to kill him had become official.

Calvary was already taking shape. Indications were that Thomas had not been far wrong when he predicted that the return of Jesus to Bethany might lead to his death (vv. 8, 16).

SUGGESTED ACTIVITIES FOR DEPTH STUDY

1. Since John tells us the purpose which determined his selection of miracles for his record (20:30–31), a rewarding study is to examine each miracle to see how it relates to the purpose of presenting Jesus as God come in the flesh. The study may be recorded in chart form. Note that the study here is of the miracle itself. Study of the discourses following a number of these miracles is reserved for a later chapter.

Miracle	Place and Circumstances	Teaching Inherent in the Miracle
(See list in chapter outline.)		(List here some ways in which the miracle was a sign, or proof, of the deity of Jesus and some truths it demonstrated.)

[1] *The New Testament in the Language of the People,* (Chicago: Moody Press, 1955).

CHAPTER 5

I. THE GOOD SHEPHERD (10:1–6, 11–18, 27–29)
  1. The Nature of the Shepherd
  2. The Benefits the Sheep Enjoy

II. THE DOOR (10:7–9)
  1. The Only Entrance
  2. Full Protection

III. THE BREAD OF LIFE (6:48–58)

IV. THE LIGHT (8:12)
  1. Functions of Light
  2. Jesus As Light

V. ETERNAL DEITY (8:56–59)

VI. THE WAY (14:1–6)

VII. THE TRUTH (14:6)
  1. Nature of Truth
  2. Truth Incarnate

VIII. THE TRUE VINE (15:1–8)
  1. A Living Union
  2. Tragedy of Separation

IX. THE RESURRECTION AND THE LIFE (11:25; 14:6)
  1. He Lived
  2. He Died
  3. He Lives

X. CONCLUSION

5

Jesus' Claims for Himself

John 10:1–18, 27–29; 6:48–58; 8:12, 56–59;
14:1–6; 15:1–8; 11:25

JESUS' TEACHING SKILLS are nowhere more aptly applied than
in his use of figures of speech. He was a master of the terse
metaphor and analogy as well as the more lengthy parable.
Although John makes little reference to Jesus' parables, he
includes many metaphors and analogies that the Master
used to convey claims about himself. John could bear no
better witness to his Lord than to share these self-revelations
of Jesus.

The "I am's" of Jesus recorded in John's Gospel have often
been noted. As we study these one by one, we shall see that
in each figure of speech Jesus unfolded fresh truth about
himself. Each metaphor emphasizes some phase of Jesus'
mission in the lives of men. Thus, in the blending of color-
ful figures of speech, we come to see the self-portrait of the
matchless Messiah.

I. THE GOOD SHEPHERD (10:1–6, 11–18, 27–29)

We begin our study of the "I am's" of Jesus with one of his
most appealing claims, "I am the good shepherd" (10:11,
14). This assertion was a high point in the lessons he taught
after healing the man born blind. (Will you pause to read
John 10:1–6, 11–18, 27–29 in a favorite translation?)

1. *The Nature of the Shepherd*

Jesus knew the practices of pastoral Palestine. Sheep and

shepherds were numerous, and relationships between them were well known and beautiful. Jesus grasped and used a familiar situation. In doing so he gave to his followers comforting and assuring truths about himself.

A true shepherd loves his sheep. Note the tender words, "He calleth his own sheep by name." "The sheep . . . know his voice." "I . . . know my sheep, and am known of mine." Since sheep were kept largely for wool, they usually enjoyed a long association with their shepherd, who developed deep love for his sheep. The shepherd's call was well known to the sheep, and they associated it with the tenderness and care of the one who provided for them. Thus, the analogy of the shepherd brought to the minds of Jesus' hearers many truths they could easily grasp.

Reference to the shepherd must have brought to many hearers memories of Psalm 23. Thus, Jesus was showing his likeness to, and his oneness with, the Father. The full provision, the still waters, the green pastures, the sure guidance, all are involved in the Good Shepherd figure. Even the rod and the staff reflect the shepherd's care, since they are used for the good of the sheep.

The true shepherd unhesitatingly risks his life for his sheep. He faces danger routinely to provide them safety. Without the shepherd, the sheep are helpless. Unlike many other animals, sheep have no sense of direction. The lost sheep must be restored to the fold by someone who knows the way. The dangers of mountain steeps were well known, but the shepherd thinks not of himself. He is always on duty. The welfare of his sheep always takes priority. Wild animals must be met and mastered. Anyone who wishes to scatter the sheep to destroy them must first overcome the shepherd, because he is the main protection for the sheep.

2. *The Benefits the Sheep Enjoy*

Blessed are those who follow the true Shepherd. This is

a lasting as well as a rewarding relationship. As you read verses 27–29 note that the statements are all connected by "and's," thus suggesting the idea that the full measure of blessings and the assurance of security follow like a chain reaction when the sheep give complete trust and allegiance to their Shepherd.

II. THE DOOR (10:7–9)

Describing himself in another way, Jesus said, "I am the door." This figure is related to the shepherd's work, but in another sense. Two types of shepherds were known. One was the keeper of a large, permanent enclosure into which all sheep of the community were gathered. Herds were combined for overnight protection, and one shepherd was fixed with responsibility to care for them all.

The other system of tending sheep was probably the one to which Jesus referred. In this case, the shepherd's individual protection was given his own sheep far from home. After the sheep were enclosed, he personally became the living door, even sleeping across the entrance to the fenced-in area. In this way he provided living guardianship for his sheep.

1. *The Only Entrance*

The figure of the door also suggests entrance. Men do not enter God's kingdom by holding to certain ethical codes, committing themselves to particular theological views, or being loyal to some ecclesiastical system—wonderful as these are. It is Jesus who is the entrance way, and there is no other. Salvation lies in meeting him, not in baptism or morality. Jesus is not like a lifeless door that can be opened by the push of another. Jesus is the living door. Nothing comes in or goes out without his personal will, knowledge, and permission. His individual care is shown by his constant attention. No greater security can be known than that which believers know in him.

Our bond of unity with other sheep of the fold (10:16) is found in him. At the time John wrote, many Jewish Christians were still finding it hard to accept the truth that believers of other races or nations were in the fold, also.

2. *Full Protection*

As the door, Jesus not only provides the entrance for the sheep; he bars the way to devouring beasts that would enter to destroy them. No animal could touch the sheep without first overpowering the shepherd. Even so, Jesus presents himself not only as our Saviour, but also as our keeper. How helpless his followers would be in life's battles were it not for his constant protecting hand.

The door not only keeps wild animals out, it keeps the sheep in until the shepherd moves forth with them and ahead of them (v. 4). No lamb could wander away without the knowledge of the shepherd. It is Jesus' desire to prevent the roaming and straying of his own into hazardous and hurtful paths. The constant alertness of the Saviour is one of the most thrilling assurances in Jesus' revelation of himself as door and shepherd.

III. THE BREAD OF LIFE (6:48–58)

The teaching about the Bread of life followed the feeding of the five thousand. Men were more concerned for material benefits than for the truths that Jesus set forth. As we shall see in chapter 6, Jesus used this problem situation as a teaching opportunity. What did he mean when he claimed, "I am the living bread"?

Having entered the door to the fold and having placed himself in the care of the Good Shepherd, the believer experiences Christ in the relationship implied in the figure of Bread of life. Meditate on some truths implied in this figure. As the Bread of life, Christ is nurture for the believer, essential to life, and the source of strength for the task.

Food is not just for pleasure, but for nurture. It enters the bloodstream. It becomes the very marrow and bones of being. Jesus holds just such a relationship to his followers. Faith brings nurture to the soul, even as eating brings strength to the body. Jesus was speaking in a practical sense. He is the source of life's strength.

Food is one of life's essentials in the physical realm. In the spiritual realm, the best and noblest of men need Christ, the Bread of heaven. In this sense, everyone suffers malnutrition until he receives heaven's nurture. There can be no spiritual life without food from above. Such food is not an option; it is a necessity. Living Bread is more needed than physical food or warm clothing. Jesus Christ is just that essential. He is life's greatest necessity.

Proper spiritual food not only prevents malnutrition; it provides the means of spiritual growth and strength. As you read John 6:53–58, preferably in several translations, note the results that follow the continuing experience of feeding on Christ.

In spite of man's needs and Jesus' adequacy, there are men who will decline his generosity. "This is the bread which cometh down from heaven, that a man may eat thereof, and not die" (v. 50). Yet there are still those who ask "How?" (v. 52). They refuse the explanation which Jesus has given: "He that eateth my flesh, and drinketh my blood, dwelleth in me, and I in him" (v. 56).

IV. THE LIGHT (8:12)

We have already noted, in the prologue to John's Gospel, the references to Jesus as light (1:4–9). Jesus, in his dealing with the case of the woman taken in adultery, showed the blackness of hidden sin in the hearts of the scribes and Pharisees who accused her (8:1–11). Following this incident Jesus identified himself as the Light of the world, and thereby claimed to fulfil functions comparable to those of light.

1. *Functions of Light*

As darkness conceals, so light reveals. Darkness is the symbol of error and evil; light is the symbol of goodness and truth. In darkness man cannot see, and he falters. In light man sees, so he can know security. In darkness man despairs. He is somewhat like a soldier, terror ridden at night, with bayonets all about and not one ray of light to reveal the enemy's location. Worse than any midnight is the moral darkness of unbelieving men. Worse than the bayonets of any army are the wages of sin.

Light shines in the darkness; it cannot go unseen. Light does not work by isolation, but by penetration. Its beam can be as slender as the finger of light from an airport beacon or as encompassing as the rays of the sun.

Light is gentle and warm. It does not work like a bulldozer, a marching army, or a fire siren. It works quietly like gravity, but it is effective.

2. *Jesus as Light*

Jesus meets men's spiritual needs as light meets their physical needs. More, he challenges his followers to receive his light and in turn become light to others. Jesus reminds us that to be givers of light we must first be recipients of light. Having received light, the Christian is under obligation to share and to spread it. "Ye are the light of the world," is the admonition of Jesus, showing the Christlikeness expected of the Master's men. The world will never be redeemed through Christians who withdraw themselves from its need and shirk their Christian obligation to provide a God-given witness.

It is tragic that blind hearts fail to discern the light of Christ's love, and therefore reject him. But denying the existence of the sun does not obliterate it. How glorious the discovery that Jesus came to be light that we may have light and therefore illuminate the paths of others. Jesus assures us: "He that followeth me shall not walk in darkness, but shall have the light of life" (8:12).

V. ETERNAL DEITY (8:56–59)

Throughout the record of Jesus' discourse in John 8, we can trace the growing rejection of the light. The religious leaders sought to rebuff Jesus. They seem continually to have shuttered every window through which any shaft of spiritual light might enter their hearts and minds.

The intellectual ambush prepared by the Jews for Jesus was swept aside by the blazing truth of his divine declaration. He reminded them of Abraham's vision of the coming Messiah, and identified himself as the subject of that prophecy. They were truly perplexed. They wondered how Abraham could have rejoiced to see Jesus' day (vv. 56–57).

Jesus gave his answer in a way that they could not misunderstand: "Before Abraham was, I am." How like the name of God given to Moses as assurance of the divine presence, when he was being called to lead the people of Israel out of their bondage (Ex. 3:14). Jesus was declared greater than Moses (1:17). In answer to the question, "Who do you claim to be?" (8:53, Williams) Jesus declared himself greater than Abraham. He claimed pre-existence to Abraham. Since God alone is timeless, Jesus was again claiming deity as he asserted his own changelessness.

This avowal, which the Jews interpreted as blasphemy, led to an effort to stone Jesus. They felt he had gone too far when he claimed superiority over their hero and ancestor. Jesus' testimony that he existed before time was and that he would abide after time ceased pierced the very hearts and consciences of the Jews. Enraged, they sought to kill him because they could not answer him.

The lesson of this entire experience is that the eternal God revealed himself to men in Jesus Christ and that Jesus came as God in human form. He is divine. As such he is "the same yesterday, and to day, and for ever" (Heb. 13:8) and "he ever liveth to make intercession" (Heb. 7:25). His incomparable place in the plan of God for human redemption rests on his eternal deity.

VI. THE WAY (14:1-6)

In his discourse with his disciples after the meal in the upper room, Jesus said, "I go to prepare a place for you. . . . Where I am, there ye may be also." Thomas posed a problem: "We know not whither thou goest; and how can we know the way?" In reply, Jesus stated the familiar threefold claim: "I am the way, the truth, and the life: no man cometh unto the Father, but by me."

Ancient religious men frequently spoke of "the way." The concept appears often in the Old Testament Scriptures, as in Psalm 27:11, "Teach me thy way, O Lord." Life is depicted as a journey and man a pilgrim walking in the way of eternal destiny. Building on that idea, Jesus identified himself as the way to God's eternal home.

The Master is not a guidepost but the guide. He does not merely point out the way. He is the "new and living way" into the presence of God (Heb. 10:20). "Through him we . . . have access . . . unto the Father" (Eph. 2:18).

Jesus Christ does not just tell men how to go; he shows where they are to walk and leads in the way. Never does he ask others to walk in paths unfamiliar to him. Not once does he stand aside just to give direction, but he invites others to follow in his footsteps. He does more. He gives life and becomes the indwelling presence who provides strength for righteous living.

He knows every step, every challenge, every pitfall of life's pathway. So he steers us from the wrong path into the right. His finger beckons, and his hand guides us. Jesus is wonderful, not only because of what he provides *for* us, but because of the things he leads us *from*. He is a necessary presence; without him our feet would falter on forbidden paths. Without him men turn "every one to his own way" (Isa. 53:6).

Thomas had wondered and asked about the way. He had expressed concern when Jesus said, "Whither I go ye know, and the way ye know" (14:4). From the Master's reply, Thomas knew he had only to follow in the footsteps of Jesus, and all would be well. Jesus was, and is, not just *a* way, but *the* way. All men are destined for eternal punishment without his guiding hand, flawless example, saving grace, and indwelling presence.

VII. The Truth (14:6)

The word "truth" is frequently used by John. Truth is an abstraction, but Jesus made it concrete and practical. In his statement, "I am . . . the truth," he calmly claimed that he embodied truth. He lived truth and made truth live. (Cf. 1: 14.) Because Jesus is the truth, he can be depended upon to be the secure way.

1. *Nature of Truth*

Truth is of divine origin. But God is invisible to the eyes. Men may yearn to see the spiritual, but such is invisible. Jesus came from the Father to reveal what God is like—to reveal to man what truth is, its source and origin. Being from God, truth is eternal. Men slew Jesus because he loved and lived the truth. They killed him, but they could not slay the truth he proclaimed and personified.

2. *Truth Incarnate*

Truth never conflicts with itself. It forms a clear and beautiful pattern. If truth in any area is fully known, it harmonizes with all other truth everywhere. Truth in any field is in accord with truth in every other field.

There was no conflict in Jesus, God's Son. He was as constant as numbers in mathematics. But whereas mathematical truth may be taught in abstraction, moral truth must be taught by example.

More than a mathematician who left a textbook for others to read, Jesus left his life for others to admire, emulate, and partake of. He is our ideal. He is more; he is our Saviour and our new life within. "The Word was made flesh," and he was "full of grace and truth" (1:14).

VIII. THE TRUE VINE (15:1–8)

By many figures of speech Jesus had sought to teach his disciples their necessary dependence on him and his complete adequacy for all their needs. When he said, "I am the vine," he added, "Ye are the branches." In this figure he set forth an abiding relationship.

1. *A Living Union*

Palestine, being mountainous, was a land in which vines thrived. Because Jesus' hearers knew the nature of vines, they immediately saw and knew the figure of speech he was using. They understood that healthy vines were necessary if connected branches were to bear productively. Never can a spiritual harvest come without a living, life-giving relationship between Christ, who is the vine, and the branches. This relationship is precisely what conversion provides for the sinner, a vital connection essential to life and fruit-bearing.

The inability of the branch to produce its own life and nourishment needs emphasis. The believer who allows his fellowship with Christ to be marred limits his fruitfulness. Like the branch whose fruit is meager or of poor quality, he must be "pruned" to be made more fruitful (v. 2).

The one who abides in Christ bears much fruit. Yet it is

Christ who gives the increase. The vine's greatest expression of genuineness is what it is able to produce through the branches. Jesus magnified this fact. What greater glory does Christ have than in producing Godlike men through his own life-giving power in them?

2. *Tragedy of Separation*

If branches do not bear, they bring disappointment. How much they are like church members who profess but who do not practice. If professing Christians do not produce fruit, does not their barrenness suggest that they have no actual connection with the vine?

Fruitless branches are pruned away, destined to die. "Apart from me ye can do nothing" (v. 5, ASV).

IX. THE RESURRECTION AND THE LIFE (11:25; 14:6)

What may be considered the climactic "I am" of Jesus was stated first to Martha while Lazarus was still in the grave. Later, Jesus included the same claim in his statement to Thomas and the other disciples. "I am the resurrection, and the life" (11:25). "I am . . . the life" (14:6). This claim gave special significance and meaning to Jesus' ministry. (Cf. 1:4.) The words said in connection with the raising of Lazarus from the dead were said also in prophecy of Jesus' own approaching death and as a forecast of what he could do for others.

1. *He Lived*

Without having lived, one certainly cannot experience a resurrection. As life must precede death, so life and death must precede the resurrection. In coming to earth to live as a man, Jesus "emptied himself" (Phil. 2:7, ASV). If he were to be the Redeemer, it was necessary that he be human as well as divine. It was imperative that he be the Son of God, but it was also necessary that he be man. So he came to dwell among men, that God's purposes might be accomplished through men who believe on him. Jesus lived.

2. *He Died*

There is no doubting his death. Even as Jesus was talking to Martha, his death was certainly impending. Prophets had predicted it; the Bible had revealed it; and Jesus foretold it. In spite of all Jesus did to forewarn his disciples, they were unprepared. Tragic injustice such as that which brought about his death was hard for men with any sense of right to comprehend. No wonder his disciples found difficulty in perceiving it. Jesus died.

3. *He Lives*

Jesus' resurrection is made all the more glorious by the type of death he had to die. After evil had done its worst, his resumption of life gave evidence beyond dispute that all his claims were true and that all his teachings should be heard and heeded.

The triumphant truth that Jesus provides believers with resurrection from the dead lifts men to shouting ground. Jesus not only arose as the "resurrection and the life," but he is the provider of eternal life to all who seek and follow him in faith. This is fact. This is Jesus' witness to us and our witness to the world. Jesus lives again. Because he lives, believers in him shall live also.

X. CONCLUSION

In other places Jesus used the words, "I am he" (John 4:26; 8:24, 28; 13:19; 18:5, 6, 8) and "I am the Son of God" (10:36). The words appear to be a direct assertion of his messianic character and mission and a claim to his deity.

All such passages show Jesus as the noble Christ. Revelation of himself is clear. Having heard his teachings, it was by deliberate rejection of Jesus that men failed to follow him. He had taught with clarity, so they had no excuse for the rejection that would forever be their own responsibility.

SUGGESTED ACTIVITIES FOR DEPTH STUDY

1. You may wish to form nine study teams. Each team will be asked to take one of the "I am's" of Jesus discussed in this chapter. Allow a few minutes for each group to refresh their memory of previous study by scanning the designated Scripture passages and the discussion in this book. Then each team should prepare a brief statement to make to the class, telling the figure of speech used and the specific aspect of Jesus' ministry to men that this figure of speech points up. Encourage them to share the devotional thoughts implied in the figure.

2. You may wish to examine some other passages in John's Gospel to determine if they contain significant "I am's." (See those listed under "Conclusion.") What aspect of Jesus' nature is portrayed in each of these claims?

CHAPTER 6

6

Truth Taught Through Problem Situations

John 2:13–22; 5:16–47; 6:15, 26–71

EARLY IN HIS ministry Jesus was addressed as "a teacher come from God" (3:2). On the last night with his disciples before the crucifixion he said, "Ye call me, Teacher, and Lord: and ye say well; for so I am" (13:13, ASV).

From the manger to the ascension, Jesus' life abounded in teaching opportunities. We are familiar with his use of such opportunities as the visit from Nicodemus or the interview with the woman of Samaria. He was always the gracious, compassionate teacher for any person who was willing to be a sincere learner. But his teaching went beyond that. In the midst of frustration, rejection, and refusal of the truth, Jesus nevertheless turned the situation into an opportunity for revelation of himself to his disciples. The adamant hearts of his enemies refused instruction, but always there was truth for all onlookers and listeners if they were willing to learn and to obey the truth.

John's witness to Jesus reveals the incomparable skill of the Master Teacher to turn the most unlikely circumstance into a learning situation. Time and again the opposition of the Jewish leaders placed Jesus in a dilemma. By consummate wisdom and skill, he not only faced the antagonism, but actually turned the attacks into opportunities to teach the disciples—and any in his audience who were willing to be taught. We select for study four instances in which Jesus turned man's unreceptiveness and deception into an opportunity for revelation of himself and of eternal truth.

I. THE SON WITH AUTHORITY OVER THE HOUSE OF HIS FATHER (2:13–22)

Jesus encountered a problem situation as he came to Jerusalem for the Passover feast (the first recorded by John). The Temple was the focal point of worship, symbolizing the whole Jewish religious system. Yet this very Temple was being grossly misused. The conditions so belied the true meaning of the Passover feast that he who had come to be our Passover Lamb could not remain silent.

1. *Prevailing Practices* (2:13–14)

The Passover was the time for payment of the Temple tax, which every mature man was assessed—an amount often equivalent to two days' wages for a laboring man. Such taxes supported the Temple sacrifices.

Although the moneys of most nations—Greek, Roman, Egyptian, or Phoenician—were usable in ordinary commerce, the Temple taxes had to be paid in certain Jewish coins. Hence, foreign moneys had to be exchanged for use in the Temple. Had the money-changers served their function unselfishly, they could have rendered the masses a very necessary service. But, in their uncontrolled profiteering, they frequently charged a poor man a whole day's wages just for exchanging coins for payment of his Temple tax. Avarice bred exploitation. No wonder the sensitive soul of Jesus was shocked when he witnessed extortion carried on even in the house of prayer and in the name of religion.

The problem was compounded because the sellers of oxen, sheep, and doves were also stationed in the Temple area to provide animals for sacrifice. This, too, could have been a helpful service had the purpose not been perverted. The animals had to be unblemished and declared perfect. Many pilgrims came from great distances, perhaps for a once-in-a-lifetime act of Temple worship. To secure sacrificial animals that had been declared perfect by the inspector, the worshiper was required to pay whatever price the seller asked. This system not only made extortion possible, but exploited the very pilgrims who could least afford it. Such entrenched evil and semilegal blackmail carried on in the name of religion inflamed Jesus to indignation.

2. *Gross Injustice* (2:16)

The mercenary motives of these money-changers desecrated the Temple in Jesus' eyes. Reverence fled the hearts of worshipers who had been met with injustice instead of solemnity. Prayer could not grow out of an emotion of resentment, and worshipers could not have a deep sense of God's presence under such circumstances. The court, which was the only place a Gentile could enter, had become more like a stockyard than a place of prayer. How could even the most sincere seekers worship amid such confusion and deception?

3. *Demonstrated Authority* (2:15–16)

Jesus took cords and made a whip as he planned to evict greedy men and expose their wrong. His act was not an impulsive one, but premeditated. He drove money lovers from the places of their money-making in the Temple, and he did it by himself. To separate a group of schemers from their spoils and to do it alone showed the amazing man that Jesus was. The words "my Father's house" showed his claim to authority. He must have been dynamic in physique and personality as well as forceful in spirit. No wonder witnesses to this event were awed by his presence. Never before had they seen Jesus in this vigorous role.

4. *Diverse Reactions* (2:17–22)

Different reactions immediately followed Jesus' violent act. Note the contrast as you read verses 17–18. The disciples, favoring what they saw, thought of Psalm 69:9, "The zeal of thine house hath eaten me up," and they counted this a fulfilment of ancient prophecy. Thus, they began to recognize that Jesus' authority over the Temple was based on the Scriptures, and on his claim that God was his Father (see v. 16).

The reaction of the leaders of the Jews was quite the opposite. They demanded a sign, credentials, proof that Jesus had legitimate authority for the drastic steps he had taken. Jesus stated a sign—the sign of his own death and resurrection (v. 19), but only later did even his disciples grasp the full implications of his reply and come to full belief (v. 22).

Jesus stated that his deity—and therefore his jurisdiction over the Temple—would be proved by his resurrection. In a sense he was making the claim, "All authority hath been given unto me," even as he declared later (Matt. 28:18, ASV). In essence Jesus said, "Kill me, and in three days I will rise from the dead" (v. 19), as he gave clear-cut authorization for what he did. So far removed from spiritual insights were his critics that they thought he was speaking of the Temple of stone in Jerusalem. They failed to comprehend that he was referring to the temple of his own body.

5. *Spiritual Truths*

What did Jesus mean to teach by this dramatic cleansing? Certainly, by it he declared his authority as the Son over the Temple—his Father's house.

Some Bible students feel that Jesus by his act was implying that the whole ancient system of animal sacrifices had fulfilled God's original purpose and was now about to be replaced by something far more significant. Jesus himself was the Lamb of God, and he was cleansing the Temple so that worship there might be acceptable in God's sight.

It has been further suggested that Jesus was predicting the complete demolition of the Temple by hostile enemies. Also, he was forecasting the truth that he, as the risen Christ, would be temple enough for everyone and that men could come to God by him. Thus, he revealed that no earthly temple was necessary for men to approach God.

Men with spiritual insight could see in Jesus' action certain principles:

1. The true observance of the Passover called for hearts cleansed from avarice and injustice. Men who where enslaved by greed could not meaningfully participate in the feast which celebrated their release from bondage.

2. No practice must be permitted which made it difficult for those who came to God's house to have an attitude of worship.

3. The symbolism of the Temple foreshadowed the true way to God. Jesus would fulfil that symbolism in the temple of his body.

II. THE SON, THE SOURCE OF LIFE (5:16–47)

Another problem situation developed as a sequel to the healing of the lame man at the pool of Bethzatha (Bethesda). (Please read again the account in John 5:1–16. The miracle itself was considered in your study of chapter 4.)

When the healed man identified the healer as the one who had ordered him to take up his bed and walk, he involved Jesus in a sabbath-breaking charge. This situation put Jesus under severe condemnation before his accusers, who were already seeking grounds for attack. They "sought to slay him, because he had done these things on the sabbath day."

In reply, Jesus stated again the relationship upon which all his claims rested, "My Father is working until now, and

I Myself am working" (5:17, NASB). The accusers were enraged. In their way of thinking, Jesus had added blasphemy to sabbath-breaking, since by his statement he was making himself equal with God.

Such a situation of prejudice, tension, and anger gave the setting for Jesus' teaching of a profound truth—the truth that, as the Son of God, he was and is the source of life. The discourse is one of the longer ones of John's Gospel. Through years of reflection John's insights into these truths had been quickened. From a heart and mind made ready by inspiration, the apostle recorded these words that others might know what the Holy Spirit had made them mean to him.

1. Shocking Claims (5:17–29)

As you read verses 17–29, note the repeated use of the terms "the Son" and "the Father." Jesus was making claims about himself which seemed preposterous to his audience of haughty unbelievers, but he was doing it in the light of the Scriptures and the Jews' own traditions. To comprehend how subtly Jesus was instructing his hearers, we must see the working of the Jewish mind.

(1) *Claim to be one with the Father.*—Jesus was making claims which only God can make. His hearers caught what he was saying as he claimed functions and powers which had been ascribed to the Messiah. Unmistakably, he was avowing that he was the Chosen One of God, the Messiah, the Anointed One. These were deliberate, purposeful declarations. Then and there Jesus had performed the miracle of healing to substantiate his claim.

(2) *Claim to be the giver of eternal life.*—Jesus' claims were shocking to his enemies. In their frustration they launched a brutal attack. Having identified himself, Jesus proceeded to speak of the Father-Son relationship (vv. 19–23). He made the acceptance of himself as the Messiah tantamount to receiving eternal life (v. 24) and implied

that those who rejected him subjected themselves to eternal judgment (v. 29).

(3) *Claim to be the fulfilment of prophecy.*—The term "Son of man" (v. 27) is significant. Actually, this was a strong messianic title. Daniel had referred to "one like the Son of man" who was coming with power and unto whom would be given "dominion, and glory, and a kingdom," which would be "an everlasting dominion, which shall not pass away, and his kingdom that which shall not be destroyed" (Dan. 7:13-14).

By applying the term, "the Son of man," to himself, Jesus claimed to be the promised deliverer foretold by Daniel. Even his critics, knowing the hidden meanings and backgrounds, understood what he was saying.

Isaiah had predicted the healing of the lame (Isa. 35:6). At the pool of Bethzatha, Jesus had healed the lame man, and his critics had seen it. No wonder these legalists were furious. The Scriptures were being fulfilled before their very eyes. They were powerless to give rebuttal.

2. *Irrefutable Testimony* (5:30-39, 46)

Jesus summoned witnesses to testify to the truth of his claims. John the Baptist had borne testimony to him (vv. 32-35). Jesus asserted, "The very works that I do, bear witness of Me, that the Father has sent Me (v. 36, NASB). He further declared: "The Father himself, which hath sent me, hath borne witness of me" (v. 37). "The scriptures . . . testify of me" (v. 39). "Moses . . . wrote of me" (v. 46). John the Baptist, the miracles, the Father, the Scriptures, Moses himself—unanimously these witnesses converge on one point of truth: Jesus was God in the flesh.

That fact takes ascendancy over all other truth. It is the main emphasis of John's Gospel, the burden of his message to men. To overlook this point in the Gospel of John is to miss the meaning of all that the writer was trying to give.

Bypass this truth in the Bible and all else becomes distorted —even the world about becomes topsy-turvy as life loses balance and meaning.

As the divine Son of God, Jesus is the hub of the wheel of the universe, the articulating point of history. As Paul later put it, "By him all things consist" (Col. 1:17). In other words, by him all things are held together and properly relate to each other. Yet this divine one had become man.

3. *Pending Condemnation* (5:40–47)

Jesus perplexed the Jews even more by telling them that they were disobeying and denying Moses' teachings when they refused to accept Jesus, since Moses had told of him and of his coming. The scribes and Pharisees, who grasped for praise from men, received the greater condemnation for their own unbelief.

As you read verses 40–47 note the pathos in the "not's" Jesus mentions: "Ye will not come." "Ye have not the love of God." "Ye receive me not." "Ye . . . seek not the honour that cometh from God." "Ye believe not his [Moses'] writings." Their sinning against so much light made theirs an even more terrible rejection. The privileges which they had spurned increased their guilt.

Not only are unbelievers eternally condemned, but in their lives are numerous deficiencies and complexities. Disbelief loses them their all. Without faith and love, life has little of joy and meaning. Faith, by contrast, awakens a response in men, challenging them to their best. An eternity of difference is born when men trust Jesus.

III. THE SON, THE SUSTAINER OF LIFE (6:15, 26–59)

The great Galilean campaign of Jesus made marvelous history, but it collapsed when he refused the insistence of the clamorous crowd that he become their earthly king.

1. *Clamor for a Beneficent King* (6:15)

The spontaneous support of the people who had shared in the miracle of the feeding of the five thousand took the form of a movement to make Jesus king. Apparently they concluded that if he were king they could cease their labors and give their full time to more pleasant things. Later, when Jesus and the disciples were on the other side of the Sea of Galilee, the crowds thronged him again. Jesus regretted their insistence and sought to explain to them their error in judgment. As you read verse 26 think how sad the Master's tone must have been.

2. *The Misunderstood Miracle* (6:26)

Miracles were used by Jesus for instruction. They were really parables being enacted. To the earnest disciples the meaning became clear. But the message of Jesus was not grasped by the materially minded. The people had seen what he did as he fed the multitude, but they missed the spiritual lessons completely.

The people saw bread held in the hand of Jesus, but they failed to see Jesus as the Bread of heaven. They saw loaves and fishes, but they failed to see Jesus as the one who would nurture and sustain spiritual life. Being interested in filling their own stomachs, they had missed the opportunity to fill their souls.

We have already discussed the miracle of feeding the multitude (chap. 4) and the significance of Jesus' presentation of himself as the Bread of life (chap. 5). Now we are focusing attention on the discouraging situation which resulted from the dullness and antagonism with which many of the hearers met this teaching. We are giving emphasis to how Jesus met this problem and turned it into a learning experience for all of his followers who had teachable hearts.

3. *True Manna from Heaven* (6:27–59)

Jesus answered the desire of men for a freedom from their labors by giving a new definition of work: "This is the work of God, that ye believe on him whom he hath sent" (v. 29). The Jews required a sign, citing the giving of the manna (Ex. 16:15) as an illustration of the kind of sign they wanted. Unwilling to admit that the feeding of the five thousand was sufficient evidence, they challenged Jesus to produce bread from heaven to prove his claim. The reply of Jesus reminded them that Moses had not given the manna; God gave it. Thus Jesus made even the heckling of his opponents an opportunity to reveal himself as the sustainer of life.

The Jews not only failed to believe, but they began to argue among themselves (v. 52) about the meaning of Jesus' teachings and possibly the truth of what he was saying. They heard but they did not learn. For their made-up minds his words were hard to understand. In response, Jesus expanded his teaching in a discourse that proved exceedingly puzzling to his hearers. Read verses 53–58 in a modern translation and imagine hearing these words for the first time.

So Jesus said to them: "Unless you do eat the body of the Son of Man and drink his blood, you are not really living at all. The man who eats my flesh and drinks my blood has eternal life and I will raise him up when the last day comes. For my body is real food and my blood is real drink. The man who eats my body and drinks my blood shares my life and I share his. Just as the living Father sent me and I am alive because of the Father, so the man who lives on me will live because of me. This is the bread which came down from Heaven! It is not like the manna which your forefathers used to eat, and died. The man who eats this bread will live for ever" (Phillips).[1]

These were the words of self-revelation which Jesus gave in the synagogue at Capernaum (v. 59). He was seeking

---

[1] From *The New Testament in Modern English*, © J. B. Phillips, 1958. Used with permission of the Macmillan Company.

to unfold the important truth that he was not given as one of life's luxuries, but rather to be life's most basic necessity.

IV. THE SON, THE DISCERNER OF DISCIPLESHIP (6:60–71)

The message of Jesus Christ inevitably tests and divides men. Faith leads to happy commitments; lack of faith leads to desertion in times of stress.

1. *Nominal Followers Tested* (6:60–66)

Having seen the "signs," many people were charmed by the obvious power and uniqueness of our Lord. They followed him spontaneously. Miracles had awakened an interest which could hardly be classified as faith. Many followers came after Jesus out of curiosity. They saw the unusualness of the man but hardly comprehended the truths he was teaching. Some did grasp what Jesus meant, but, knowing that to follow his truth meant trouble, they fled in the opposite direction.

The teachings of Jesus about himself as the Bread of life caused murmuring among his followers (vv. 60–61). Jesus responded by explaining that the life he was offering was of the Spirit (vv. 62–65). People turned away en masse when they heard this saying. No doubt they realized that their hopes for an assured supply of physical bread had not materialized. Notice (vv. 67–71) how Jesus used this situation to lead the twelve to renewed commitment.

2. *Jesus' Test of His Own Disciples* (6:67)

The loneliness of abandonment cut deep into the sensitive soul of our Lord. Being human as well as divine, he lamented the departure of his former followers and turned to question his disciples: "Will ye also go away?" or, as we would put it, "You are not going to leave me, too, are you?"

Though the reasons for following Jesus might have been artificial on the part of many, they were possible learners as long as they sat at his feet. By leaving him they were losing all contact. What chance would he have with them then? Would their withdrawal make it harder for other men to listen? By asking about the sincerity and depth of conviction of his own disciples, who had followed him intimately and long, Jesus probed into their motives and responses.

3. *Peter's Noble Declaration* (6:68–69)

Peter was the one who so often spoke out of turn. Impetuous as he was, he usually spoke, then thought. Impulsive words were often wrong. But this time Peter responded both spontaneously and brilliantly. Long meditation could not have made his answer more meaningful. John, in his Gospel of witness to Jesus, was careful to record Peter's testimony.

Peter answered in the form of a question and an assertion, "Lord, to whom shall we go? thou hast the words of eternal life. And we believe and are sure that thou art that Christ, the Son of the living God." Volumes were said in these words. Peter had seen, and he now declared the truth. If man turns from Christ Jesus, there is nowhere else to go. Peter and the other true followers knew that fact. They were sure who Jesus was and why he had come. They would stand steadfastly.

4. *Judas' Defection Foretold* (6:70–71)

The most tragic prediction in this record was of the desertion of Judas. Perhaps intellectually he understood, but as he stood at the crossroads he deliberately made the wrong choice. Jesus' foreknowledge of the betrayal cut deeply, and he lamented the desertion which would come. At the same time, the Master began to prepare the other disciples for Judas' defection.

5. *Continued Testing*

John's report of Jesus as the discerner of false and true discipleship makes it clear that the claims of Christ are tests and evidences of human faith. These claims are still separating the false followers from the true. They cause many nominal Christians to turn their backs and go away, but true believers will be true to the end, whatever the cost.

Christianity is more than a philosophy for one to accept intellectually. It is a way of life that grows out of one's loving response to the Lord Jesus. Christianity is not the system of one's thoughts, it is Christ's mastery over one's life. It is life's answer to Christ's invitation, to which one gives his total self in full response.

The constant teaching of Jesus was his call to men to maximum living. By words, example, instruction, challenge, illustration, incident, influence, and any other method at his disposal, he was exalting God and interpreting Christian truth.

SUGGESTED ACTIVITIES FOR DEPTH STUDY

The problems Jesus met in his ministry would have frustrated a weak character; they would have challenged a mere crusader or reformer to sweep aside opponents. They caused Jesus to seize the opportunities to teach, and thus to seek to win even his opponents.

When this study is made in class, you may list the four problems mentioned as follows:

Dealing with commercialized religion (2:13–22)
Meeting persecution caused by spiritual blindness (5:16–47)
Dealing with opportunism in would-be followers (6:15, 26–59)
Sifting real from superficial discipleship (6:60–71)

Form four study teams. Ask each team to take one of the problems designated and to examine the Scripture reference, as they prepare to report (1) the setting and circumstances in which the problem arose, (2) how the problem showed itself, (3) the central truth or truths Jesus brought out as he faced the problem.

CHAPTER 7

7

Greatness Revealed in Opposition

John 7 : 1–52; 8 : 12–55; 10 : 22–39

IN HIS WITNESS to Jesus, John records the unbelief and open hostility which the Master faced. Against this dark background the portrait John paints stands out in relief. Jesus proclaimed truth with zeal. His life sparkled with winsomeness, bringing eyes in any crowd instantly to him.

Such stirring leadership characteristics won Jesus many friends and increased his influence on earth. But the same traits brought him many enemies. Men who felt threatened were jealous of Jesus' name and fame. They resented his influence and sought to stop his movement.

Opposition or persecution seems to be the price all men must pay for effective leadership. It is doubtful that anyone can exert profound and productive influence without stirring up strife. The same vigorous discipleship which makes friends also produces enemies. The man who is passive and afraid rarely finds either.

The detractors who sought to denounce Jesus actually helped him reveal himself more fully. Witnesses observed Jesus in awkward positions, as enemies hurled ruthless, relentless attacks against him. Did he ever show more nobility than when he was subjected to grossly unjustified attacks by unfair and untruthful men?

The men who evidently thought Jesus would either be silenced or would back down found him entrenched more deeply in the hearts of his admirers. Instead of retreating, he advanced. Rather than being silenced, his words were more carefully chosen and were golden in meaning and effect. Instead of impatience and anger, Jesus faced his opponents with tenderness and understanding.

The greatness of Jesus clearly manifested itself in each crisis, as his antagonists grew in number, accelerated their attacks, and consolidated their efforts. The teamwork of such diverse groups as Pharisees, Sadducees, and Herodians indicates how impassioned was their mutual hatred for Jesus. Though they differed on almost everything else, they could unite on their opposition to him.

Jesus came to redeem men and to give them power to be Godlike. Such a purpose was destined to arouse Satan's full forces and to stir opposition in many quarters.

I. DOUBTED BY HIS OWN FAMILY (7:1–9)

After the teaching about the Bread of life (John 6), Jesus withdrew from Judea to Galilee (7:1). By the time of the Feast of Tabernacles, the developing animosities seemed sure to force his death without delay.

As Jesus tarried in Galilee, making no move to go up to the feast, his brothers began to taunt him: "You ought to leave here and go to Judaea so that your disciples can see what you are doing, for nobody works in secret if he wants to be known publicly. If you are going to do things like this, let the world see what you are doing" (vv. 3–4, Phillips).

Were Jesus' brothers calling him a coward, or were they giving well-meant advice? Certainly they could neither understand him nor advise him aright, "for neither did his brethren believe in him."

Jesus answered simply, "My time is not yet come." When his brothers moved on to Jerusalem to attend the Feast of Tabernacles, Jesus went up also, but in a quiet, unostentatious manner. His name was on the lips of the crowds. Some sustained his greatness; others were severely critical, accusing him of misleading the people. He was fully aware of the animosity. He knew that the world hated him because he was testifying that its works were evil (v. 7).

II. FURTHER OPPOSITION IN JERUSALEM (7:10–52)

As we have seen, Jesus at first refused to go to the Feast of Tabernacles because the psychological moment had not yet arrived for him to do so (v. 8). Later the circumstances changed, and he went.

1. *Smoldering Hostility* (7:10–18)

There was excitement about Jesus' attendance at the feast, for it was rumored that surely he must be the Messiah. Although talk to this effect was abundant, it seems to have been in relatively closed circles. Apparently, those talking sensed danger in publicly proclaiming their convictions. Others present recognized that Jesus was an unusual and great man, but they were not willing to accept his messiahship.

About midway in the feast, Jesus began to teach in the Temple. His grasp of truth baffled those present, because he had not received the formal schooling which was required of religious rulers. Sensing the perplexity of his hearers, Jesus explained that his knowledge was from God. He went on to tell them that ample knowledge was available if men would only commit themselves to God. If one sincerely purposes to *do* God's will, he will be given ability to discern the truth (v. 17). (It will be interesting to read this verse in several translations.)

2. *Open Opposition* (7:19–52)

Jesus pointed out that, although his hearers claimed loyalty to the law of Moses, they were actually planning to violate the law by killing him. The question (v. 23) he hurled back at his critics caught them unprepared. They found themselves unable to answer the inquiry about their own practice of circumcision on the sabbath, while at the same time they objected to Jesus' healing of a man in entirety on a sabbath day. The reference seems to be to the healing of the man at the pool of Bethzatha, which had brought to a climax the accusation against Jesus as a sabbath breaker.

Division of opinion is shown, in that some called Jesus "a good man" (v. 12) and "the Prophet" (v. 40), while others called him a demon (v. 20), implying mental or moral blemish.

The sheer courage of Jesus in the presence of such bias and injustice was observed by some (v. 26). Friends noted his willingness to speak publicly in the presence of sneers and jeers, now that the time was right.

Jesus did give profound teachings, even though arguments raged and officials were seeking to arrest him. (Read vv. 33–36.) He predicted his death and departure, because he knew full well where this opposition would lead.

How wonderful it was that there were those present who could declare with conviction, "This is the Christ" (v. 41), as they blew aside the smoke of opposition to recognize who he was and what he had come to earth to do.

There emerged some wonderfully complimentary words, such as, "Never man spake like this man" (v. 46). In spite of the stresses of extreme fear, some people had been convinced that Jesus was God's Son, had believed, and had received Jesus' assurance of discipleship (v. 31). Nevertheless, the Pharisees lamented that others could see noble things in Jesus. They felt that those who were kind to Jesus or sympathetic to his views were being misled. Knowing that Jesus was from Galilee was enough for them, because nowhere did the Scriptures identify a noble prophet who would come from that place. So they shut their minds to truth. No one is so blind as the man who refuses to receive spiritual insight.

III. ADAMANT PREJUDICE (8:12–20)

In chapter 5 we studied Jesus' claim, "I am the light of the world" (v. 12). It is our purpose here to focus on how even man's prejudice formed a backdrop which John uses to make more vivid his witness to Jesus.

Prejudice had so beclouded the hearts of the Pharisees that they could find nothing good in Jesus. They linked him to darkness rather than light, to chaos rather than peace. So their feelings were as black as their blindness.

As you read verses 12–20 note all the things Jesus said about himself. Although the closed minds of his opponents would not receive his witness, it must have made strong impression on John and the other disciples.

1. *Accused of Making False Claims* (8:13)

Plainly the Pharisees saw Jesus as an imposter, a fraud. They said bluntly, "Thou bearest record of thyself; thy record *is not true*" [author's italics]. Thus they accused him of falsehood and misrepresentation.

In reply, Jesus clearly set forth his mission and his complete commitment to the task God had sent him to accomplish. He never lost sight of it. He knew his divine destiny and accepted it. Everything he did on earth pointed toward fulfilling that clear-cut objective.

2. *Pharisees' Rejection of Their Own Law* (8:14–20)

Jesus referred to the Mosaic law that the testimony of two witnesses was to be considered valid (Deut. 19:15). He bore witness to himself and added, "The Father that sent me beareth witness of me." What greater evidence could be given? But the Pharisees rejected it, even though they customarily accepted the testimony of two witnesses. Jesus openly avowed that they knew neither God the Father, nor him as the Messiah (v. 19). No wonder they were blind. Living in darkness, they seemed unaware of the existence of light. Especially were they strangers to the light of truth and love.

Jesus held no hostility toward such men of prejudice and unbelief; he gave only sympathy and love. But their hardened hearts were unmoved. The only reason no one seized and arrested him then was that his hour had not yet come.

IV. CHARACTER DEFAMATION (8:21–55)

As you read verses 21–55, note the direct attacks on the character and veracity of Jesus. No longer content with attacking his teachings, his enemies sought to defame his person.

The argument and debate about Jesus recorded in John 8:21–55 is not easily organized systematically. It was the sort of discussion which simply flowed, controlled by a sequence of questions, circumstances, arguments, and rebuttals. Disorganized as it seems, it has superb truth which we need to observe.

1. *Fatal Unbelief* (8:21–29)

The key to understanding this passage is verse 24: "I said therefore unto you, that ye shall die in your sins: for if ye believe not that I am he, ye shall die in your sins." Jesus voiced the conviction that man's basic trouble, in any age, is sin and that the basic sin is unbelief. These men were perplexed, but their perplexity was not brought about by their stupidity or mental limitations. They were blind sinners because their hearts refused to believe.

Jesus forewarned his hearers that he was going away. He predicted that after his departure they would recognize their error and quest for him, but that the opportunity for their repentance would then be gone: "Whither I go, ye cannot come." Man's fleeting opportunities are stressed and the necessity for entering doors when they are open is magnified. The seriousness of refusing Christ is illustrated.

Many of Jesus' hearers were baffled at the Master's words about his return to glory—the place to which they could not follow because of their own unbelief. They wondered if he were telling of plans for suicide (v. 22). What distortions unbelief brings!

2. *Rewarding Discipleship* (8:30–32)

How different were Jesus' words to those who followed him in faith in spite of the vilifications hurled at him. As doubt produces despair, so faith produces assurance. Beginning with belief, discipleship opens the way to freedom in expanding knowledge of the truth. (Cf. 1:14, 17.)

The man who believes receives much, but he does not immediately receive all that Jesus has to give. Certainly, he does not receive everything in the first moment of his commitment of life. Other experiences follow, and additional blessings await him as he grows in Christian grace. Continuing or abiding in the Word (v. 31) is evidence of the genuineness of discipleship. Doubtful indeed is the discipleship of one who continually neglects, or even worse, seeks to discredit the Word of God.

In response to their faith and commitment, Christ gives his followers opportunity to know the truth—truth about life's origin, meaning, and destiny. Such truth will help one discern between the essential and the trivial. The end result is freedom. The words, "The truth shall make you free" (v. 32), are often quoted; but how often are they believed? Often they are taken out of context. Note how they relate to verse 31. Man all too frequently seeks to preserve his freedoms through force rather than truth. There is no such thing as freedom until men are first unloosed from their binding sins.

3. *Slavery and Freedom* (8:33–41*a*)

In the midst of insults, Jesus used every opportunity to offer true freedom. Even in our glorious America, which we call the land of the free, many enslaved men dwell. They are servants of alcohol, in bondage to lust, chained by greed, shackled by hate—indeed, downcast slaves of sin. True freedom—freedom of spirit—is something governments cannot give. It is available for every man, but it comes from God alone through his Son. (See v. 36.)

Even the descendants of Abraham, who prided themselves in their heritage and freedom, were slaves of sin, and they found sin a severe taskmaster. Whoever practices sin is enslaved by sin.

A slave is very different from a son. His relationships are dissimilar, his privileges diverse. Jesus pointed out that his critics were bound by sin because they did not know God as Father. (See vv. 39–41*a*.)

Jesus defined genuine sonship, urging even his critics to claim the privilege of sonship and to receive the freedom which can come in no other way. Such freedom is not gained through family inheritance, glorious history, or rich traditions. It has to come from God through Christ. Jesus stressed that his unbelieving hearers were not the true sons of Abraham, though they bore that name.

4. *Legacy of Unbelievers* (8:41*b*–55)

Brutal abuse met Jesus in the veiled implication that he was "born of fornication" (v. 41), implying that he was an illegitimate child rather than of divine birth. In spite of the ugliness of the implication, Jesus did not answer directly. Rather, he contended that his accusers' own actions made self-evident the fact that these bitter ones did not have the same Father as he, because if God were their Father they would be expressing love for Jesus as God's Son.

Then, in straightforward explanation Jesus told them why they could not understand: "Ye are of your father the devil." In saying this, Jesus showed why they were given to lies, hate, suspicion, and deafness to spiritual things. In the words, "Because I speak the truth, ye do not believe Me" (v. 45, NASB), he showed the helplessness of their plight. They did not understand the truth because they were denying the God of truth.

John and the other disciples who were listening to this open attack on their Master must have realized that criticism is inevitable for the Christian who lives forcefully and effectively. There is an inevitable conflict between truth and falsehood because they contradict each other. Men of God know truth and feel compelled to proclaim it. Men of unbelief reject truth as error because they do not know the Christ of truth, the measuring stick by which right and righteousness become known.

The feeling of the Pharisees exploded into such fanaticism that they determined to stone Jesus to death. Even though they did not kill him then and there, murder lingered in their hearts and would ultimately find expression.

V. PHYSICAL DANGER (10:22-39)

One marvels at the way Jesus met opposition from his opponents and came away victor, even as they plotted to kill him.

1. Ensnaring Question (10:22-25)

At the last Feast of Dedication Jesus was to attend in Jerusalem, men sought to get him to proclaim publicly whether or not he was the Messiah. Knowing that such a declaration would be unwise at this point, Jesus chose to point to his own deeds as being the works of the Father, challenging his questioners to draw their own conclusions. His enemies would seek to use his oral declaration as a trap. They could not argue against his deeds.

2. *Reason for Rejection* (10:26–30)

Enemies of Jesus were searching for points of attack in the hope that they could discredit him and cripple his influence. They continued to advance their opposition by seeking to destroy confidence in his character and his integrity. Jesus told his critics that the reason for their hardness of heart was that they were not his sheep. If they had been his, they would have known a life which could not be taken from them. He exalted his disciples, stressed the security of his believers, and identified himself as being one with the Father.

3. *Deeds as Evidence* (10:31–39)

Jesus' enemies picked up stones to stone him (v. 31) but something seems to have held them back. They meant only harm to him and his cause. The accusation of blasphemy (smoldering until now) was openly made (v. 33). His opponents had the point they would use to demand his death. They sought to seize him, but he eluded them.

Once more, Jesus asserted the importance of his deeds, which were proofs of his messiahship. His plea that his hearers accept the witness of his deeds even though they were rejecting his words met deaf ears. Really, there should have been no difficulty in their accepting his assertion, "The Father is in me, and I in him" (v. 38), but they would not. Unbelief is a curtain drawn against obvious truths.

When Christians seek more to impress the world with Christian deeds than with loud but fallible words, they are following the example set by Jesus.

In spite of all unfair opposition, Jesus never lost his love for men—all men and all types of men. He never veered from his main objective. His mission to earth remained in clear focus. As the scenes of earth shifted, Jesus altered tactics and timing, but never did he change purpose nor compromise truth. In demonstrating unlimited patience, alertness to his surroundings, and persistence in his holy purpose, Jesus charted the proper course for his followers forever afterward.

SUGGESTED ACTIVITIES FOR DEPTH STUDY

Depth studies based on chapter 7 will lead the student to feel something of the pain involved in the opposition and rejection Jesus experienced.

1. Find John's first reference to Jesus' brethren (2:12). From Matthew 12:46; 13:55–56 we see that the brethren did not continue to follow Jesus. John records their unbelief (7:3–5). Apparently Jesus never during his earthly life had the joy of seeing his own brothers believe on him, although there is evidence that later they were counted among Christian leaders (1 Cor. 9:5; Gal. 1:19).

2. Trace the growth in antagonism of the religious leaders until it reached an organized plot for Jesus' death. Note the reasons for this antagonism (John 5:9–18; 7:14–24, 30–32, 45–49; 8:13–20, 48–59; 9:13–16, 22, 24; 10:31–39; 11:45–53, 57; 12:10–11, 19).

3. Using the passages already listed, note Jesus' repeated efforts to lead the rulers of the Jews to see the truth. (In some instances you may wish to read a few verses beyond the reference cited.)

4. If a committee is ready, let them report on the feasts mentioned by John. They should test their report to see if it covers the feasts mentioned in the following references: John 2:13 and 23; 5:1; 6:4; 7:2ff.; 10:22; 11:55 with 12:1; 13:1; 18:39; and 19:14, 31.

CHAPTER 8

I. THE MEANING OF LIFE AND DEATH (12:20–50)
1. The Inquiring Greeks (12:20–26)
2. The Voice from Heaven (12:27–36)
3. Condemnation of Unbelief (12:37–50)

II. DEFECTION OF AN AVOWED FOLLOWER (13:18–30)
1. Prediction (13:18–21)
2. Self-examination (13:22–25)
3. Identification (13:26–30)

III. WORDS OF ENCOURAGEMENT (Chap. 14)
1. A Home in the Father's House Assured (14:1–6)
2. The Father Revealed (14:7–11)
3. The Test of Love Made Clear (14:12–15, 21)
4. The Holy Spirit Promised (14:16–18, 26–27)
5. Jesus' Return to Earth Declared (14:28)

IV. THE DISCOURSE CONTINUED (Chaps. 15–16)
1. A Chosen People (15:14–16)
2. A Responsible People (15:17–27)
3. A People of Strength and Victory (Chap. 16)

8

Witnesses Forewarned and Strengthened

John 12:20–50; 13:18–30; 14–16

CHAPTERS 12–16 record the closing days of Jesus' ministry prior to the crucifixion. John's memory seems to have been filled with the realization that Jesus had used every possible means to prepare his disciples for the dark days ahead and to give them some foreknowledge of what they must face as the witnesses who would carry on his work.

Knowing that his disciples would meet inevitable and extreme opposition, Jesus sought to prepare them for it. He wanted not only to fortify them with assurance, but to have them experience faith in living situations. He gave them a sort of internship in acute circumstances, so they would not panic later when the forces of evil converged and made onslaught upon them.

So universal is the facing of hardship by Christ's followers even today that we are grateful for John's witness, telling something of how the Lord prepared those closest to him for the crises they would face.

I. THE MEANING OF LIFE AND DEATH (12:20–50)

Over many months, hatred toward Jesus had been building up among certain religious leaders. It was intensified by the publicity and acclaim given him in connection with the raising of Lazarus and the triumphal entry into Jerusalem. The coming sufferings of Calvary hung already like a cloud on the distant horizon. After the raising of Lazarus, the Sanhedrin (council) met and officially planned to kill Jesus (11:47–53).

In this setting, John shows how the visit of some Greeks gave Jesus an opportunity for instructing his disciples as they faced the time of his death.

1. *The Inquiring Greeks* (12:20–26)

No doubt impressed by the triumphal entry of Jesus into Jerusalem were certain Greeks who had come up to the feast to worship. Accustomed to travel, they had seen and heard many strange things, but nothing akin to what they had seen and heard about Jesus. Finding Philip, they expressed their desire to meet Jesus personally. Their words, "Sir, we would see Jesus," have been used across the centuries to express the yearning of inquiring hearts.

The Greeks, ever seekers of truth, were probably proselytes, or converts to Judaism. At any rate, they represented the Gentile world to John, and they typified the glorious outreach of Jesus to all men.

Jesus gave what seems a strange answer to the request of the Greeks. (See vv. 23–26.) In symbolic language he foretold the mission of the cross. He set forth the everlasting principle that no man is prepared to live abundantly until he is willing to lay down his very life. The grain of wheat offered a graphic illustration of the principle.

This teaching was contrary to the traditional Greek ideal of self-realization and self-gratification. The Greeks had asked a question plainly. They got a clear reply. The only way to see Jesus with discerning spiritual insight is to accept the death-life principle expressed in verses 24–26. We can imagine how impressed the disciples must have been by Jesus' reply.

The truth Jesus taught is a lesson all must learn: Real life comes through death; victory is achieved by surrender;

giving means getting. Holding produces losses; self-forgetfulness brings greatness.

Reverently we may believe that Jesus himself found this truth costly in his own experience. Read his prayer in verses 27–28.

2. *The Voice from Heaven* (12:27–36)

Those who accompanied Jesus needed convincing evidence that would forever remove from their minds all doubts about him. And they received such evidence. The voice out of heaven spoke a message which approved the deeds and actions of Jesus. Strange had been the ideas men had held about the coming Messiah. They had been reluctant about being identified with one who was so plainly predicting his own death. It took a special declaration at this point to help his disciples overcome their fears with the confidence that all would be well, whatever the circumstances. The Father gave these words of assurance through a miracle. The relationship between God the Father and Jesus the Son could not have been established any more clearly.

Jesus, of course, recoiled at the prospect of the agonies of Calvary, but he knew there was no other way to redeem sinners. Certainly, the voice from heaven meant much to the heart of Jesus, even as it did to others. In reassuring contrast to the silence of unbelieving men was heard the heart-thrilling declaration of God.

There would be magnetism in the cross. Jesus' death would draw men (v. 32). By Jesus' death, men would live. It was God's strange and mighty way of purifying an unclean humanity. Men meant it for evil; God would bring eternal good out of it.

Verse 36*b* records the end of Jesus' public ministry: "These things spake Jesus, and departed, and did hide himself from them." But his teaching among his own professed disciples continued and intensified.

3. *Condemnation of Unbelief* (12:37–50)

Why did Jesus turn from the crowd? In spite of ample evidence, many still would not believe. Facts should have convinced any unprejudiced seeker, but the biased minds of doubting men seemed frozen in unbelief. They believed not on him, even though many miracles had been worked before their very eyes (v. 37). Among the authorities who believed, cowardice stifled the confession of many (vv. 42–43).

Jesus' disciples had to know how rigid the rejection was and how hardhearted unbelief could become, even in the face of indisputable facts. They, themselves, in the months ahead, were to encounter similar wilful unbelief and rejection as their testimonies were given to others.

Claiming to be the very manifestation of God on earth, Jesus wanted it made clear that rejection of him was actually rejection of God the Father (vv. 44–48). To reject Jesus is to deny God. No one can accept God and reject Jesus. No one can accept Jesus and reject God.

Jesus himself was not condemning, for this was not his ministry on earth (v. 47); the unbeliever then and now stands self-condemned by his lack of faith. Verse 48 shows the fairness of Jesus in forewarning unbelievers of their impending destiny. He felt that his disciples should have conviction about this destiny, and he spoke in no uncertain terms. After speaking, he turned more toward the optimism of faith and the victory of belief. (Read vv. 49–50.)

II. DEFECTION OF AN AVOWED FOLLOWER (13:18–30)

Jesus sought to prepare the eleven disciples for the traitorous betrayal by Judas. John records for us the occurrence at the last Passover supper. The poignant words of Jesus recorded in verses 18–20 must have come flooding into John's memory as he recorded the experiences at the

Last Supper. Indeed the evangelist had vivid personal memories of that scene, and he shares them as he bears witness to Jesus.

1. *Prediction* (13:18-21)

Human treachery is a bitter experience, and Jesus knew it at its worst. Enemies would oppose, that was sure. But for a friend to betray would cut doubly deep. Jesus was not taken by surprise by the deceit of Judas, for he had said plainly, "One of you shall betray me." Evidently the other disciples had never known just how impure the heart of Judas was. Jesus, however, knew Judas' ulterior motives; yet, such foreknowledge did not seem to ease the sting when the display of treachery finally came.

2. *Self-examination* (13:22-25)

Although Jesus knew the heart of Judas—for no set of circumstances can deceive the Master—he did not condemn Judas publicly or directly, even when he could have done so justifiably. Love grasped at the last opportunity to reach this man and change his life in character and course. Judas may well have been one of the most brilliant of the disciples. Had his heart really been changed, he could have meant much to the Christian cause. In a very intimate and personal way Jesus sought to lead Judas out of himself and into newness of life and purpose.

The disciples listened in dismay, each examining himself in the light of Jesus' words. Matthew and Mark report that each of the disciples was asking, "Lord, is it I?"

3. *Identification* (13:26-30)

Rather than pointing his finger, Jesus identified the betrayer by dipping the morsel. Such was the usual sign of special interest or even friendship. (Cf. Ruth 2:14.) Unworthy though Judas was, Jesus was concerned about him and dealt with his needs with such delicacy that the other disciples did not grasp the meaning of Judas' hasty departure. They thought that he had gone to get some additional food or to give something to the poor. How hard must have been the heart of Judas not to have responded to the obvious displays of tenderness which Jesus' love revealed.

Judas went out, "and it was night." Indeed it was! And how dark was such a night!

III. WORDS OF ENCOURAGEMENT (Chap. 14)

The farewell discourse of the Master began in the upper room and continued as he walked with the disciples toward Gethsemane. His disciples never escaped the impact of the profound teachings received at this time. Jesus' words were relevant and urgently needed. These followers simply had to know that, even though some men would do their worst to destroy the Christ, God would bring glory to himself and life to others by the Son's death.

1. *A Home in the Father's House Assured* (14:1-6)

The yearning for life after death seems inborn in almost every man. But shall man live again? That is the question of the ages. If so, where? Jesus revealed that man's most beautiful dreams are insufficient to foresee the glory of the eternal home, where God's children will everlastingly abide. It is a place of mansions prepared by the divine hand, a place where the inseparable presence of the triune God shall be experienced.

Such assurances undoubtedly gave the disciples a growing confidence. They had bordered on despair, realizing the presence of passionate hatred and, in part, realizing the imminence of the death and departure of their Lord. How wonderful to hear—even if they could not comprehend—those words about the Father's house prepared for them.

2. The Father Revealed (14:7–11)

Men had wondered what God was like. Their eyes could not behold nor their imagination portray the invisible Father. Jesus once more asserted his oneness with the Father in character, purpose, and total identity (v. 9).

The disciples were reassured by this glorious truth. In Jesus' presence they could feel and know the divine presence. The statement, "He that hath seen me hath seen the Father," meant much to the disciples at this time.

3. The Test of Love Made Clear (14:12–15, 21)

Jesus' assertion in verse 12 is astounding. How can the believer do greater works than Jesus did? Whatever it means, the context makes clear that the motivation is love (v. 15) and the power to achieve is from the Holy Spirit (v. 16). "If ye love me, keep my commandments," is a challenge to demonstrate love with action. No doubt Judas' betrayal made this statement even more significant. Judas' words betokened love, but his deeds declared hate. Some translations give the clearer meaning: "If ye love me, ye will keep my commandments" (v. 15, ASV). What greater response can there be? Love is more than an emotion; it is a way of life.

4. The Holy Spirit Promised (14:16–18, 26–27)

Jesus assured the disciples over and over again that his coming death did not indicate that they would be forsaken. They would not be left abandoned when the Master was slain.

Devout Jews had looked forward to the coming "consolation of Israel" (Luke 2:25; cf. Isa. 40:1). Jesus came, and he proved to be just that. He brought comfort and consolation not only to those of Israel, but to all men of all nations who would look to him. But for Jesus to fulfil his mission demanded his death, since an atonement was required for forgiveness and life eternal. Death meant departure, and departure meant grief for broken hearts. It was timely for Jesus to give comfort just then.

The promise of "another Comforter" was needed (vv. 16, 26). The Holy Spirit would come to work amid Jesus' followers to extend the kingdom and to build the church which the Master began. The Spirit is God as man's helper come to earth. He would do mighty things through Jesus' own followers. Because the Comforter would come, Jesus could bestow his peace upon his own (v. 27). Such promises helped to fortify the disciples as they faced the agonizing loneliness following Jesus' departure by death. They would need a confident spirit in a stormy world.

5. *Jesus' Return to Earth Declared* (14:28)

"Ye have heard how I said unto you, I go away, *and come again unto you* [author's italics]." These words went even beyond the promise of the Spirit and led the disciples to anticipate the ultimate glorious return of their Lord to earth. This, too, was a welcome assurance. They could face hardship and heartache since they could know that these would pass away and be replaced ultimately by the radiant return and presence of their Master, with whom they might live forevermore. The gloom of the darkest night could be faced as long as they had the shining hope of the sunlight of a bright tomorrow.

No Christian can remain an effective witness without having throbbing hope within his breast. With such a living faith, the believer can endure persecution with grace and can advance with courage.

IV. THE DISCOURSE CONTINUED (Chaps. 15–16)

Talking with his disciples as he walked, Jesus missed no opportunity to instruct. They had so much to learn. Time was precious, and not one moment should be lost. Evidently, the disciples did not, at the time, recognize the full import of all that Jesus was saying, but he gave them truth that he felt they could eventually grasp. Surely their human comprehension and retention would be limited, even at best, but Jesus promised that "the Comforter, even the Holy Spirit" would teach them and "bring to . . . remembrance" what had been said (14:26, ASV). He is our teacher also, as we read these words of Jesus.

Following his use of the figure of the true vine (which we studied in a previous chap.), Jesus continued his teaching, assuring the disciples of full joy and abiding love (15:9–13).

1. *A Chosen People* (15:14–16)

As chosen ones, believers are "friends," doing the work of Jesus, responding to his wishes, demonstrating his spirit and courage. (You will wish to ponder v. 14.) Moreover, Jesus assured his disciples, "Ye have not chosen me, but I have chosen you." The eternal purpose of God is revealed in the initiative he takes in redeeming unworthy humanity.

God took every initiative in man's salvation. He chose man. Man did not choose God. Jesus, as God's Son, can say to all believers, "I have chosen you." Gladly will he link his life to theirs and theirs to his in life-giving relationship (which has already been described by the vine-branch symbol). With such a relationship, Jesus assures his own, "I have appointed you to go and bear fruit that will be lasting" (v. 16, Phillips).

2. *A Responsible People* (15:17–27)

Love for one another is a result of implanted love from above. It cannot exist without a personal experience with Jesus, for divine love must have a divine origin. It is transplanted in the hearts of men when men know God. Christians are to love one another. Such is the best evidence of faith and Christian experience. Hatred, bickering, littleness, all indicate that fellowship with Christ is broken—if it ever existed.

Christians are witnesses to the world. It is a world which hates and opposes and seeks to frustrate the purposes of God. But Christians will not become participants in the enmities of earth to which they are exposed. Christians never deal in hatred. They will meet hatred with love, knowing that light alone can overcome darkness, and that God eventually will destroy all evil.

3. A People of Strength and Victory (Chap. 16)

Jesus plainly stated the aim he had in mind in this discourse (v. 1). It was to prepare the disciples that they might not be "offended" (trapped) by the things they must face in the future.

(1) *Tribulations foretold* (16:1–4, 32).—Although the believers would be punished, even excommunicated—put out of the synagogue—they would not be destroyed or overcome. They might be murdered, but they could not be annihilated. Inevitable opposition would come from those who did not know Jesus, those who sought to destroy him and his influence. But the opposers, then and now, need also to know the Christ of love, and they need to be told of him and his goodness. Only Christians can show the world the true way, and it is not always the easy way.

(2) *The Holy Spirit again promised* (16:5–15).—Jesus expanded his teaching about the work of the Comforter. (As you read vv. 5–15 note what the Holy Spirit does for the unbeliever and what he does for the Christian.)

He who would convict men of sin, righteousness, and judgment was to be sent for a divine mission.

The Spirit convicts men of sin. Transgressors will not be pained by their transgressions until the Holy Spirit stabs them. It is then that pride turns to humility and arrogance to prayer. Preachers cannot make sinners sorry for their sin, but the Holy Spirit can and does.

The Holy Spirit convicts men of righteousness. Erring critics felt that Jesus was unrighteous and deserved to die, otherwise they would not have wanted to slay him with such violence. They thought they were honoring God by persecuting Jesus. But the Holy Spirit of God came to show men what true righteousness is. Seeing it, men had a true standard of measurement and began to be aware of their own cruel hearts.

The Holy Spirit convicts of judgment. Men cannot do evil things and escape the results. The Holy Spirit is the one who helps men to know that judgment is sure and gives them the desire to seek forgiveness for their shameful ways. No wonder the Holy Spirit is called the "Spirit of truth," for men cannot know truth apart from his teaching.

The Holy Spirit will enlighten, encourage, and empower the followers of Christ. No obstacle shall be too high, no weight too heavy, no problem too acute. God through his Holy Spirit has provided a sure way of victory for believers.

(3) *Sorrow and joy foretold* (16:16–22).—Nowhere does Jesus promise that Christians shall have easy lives or be exempt from suffering. He went so far as to say, "Ye shall be sorrowful" (v. 20). It is reassuring that Jesus did not stop at that point. He added, "But your sorrow shall be turned into joy." (As you read vv. 16–22, first find all the notes of sorrow, then all the notes of joy.)

Pain and death are to be overcome. They are not final masters. The Bread of heaven is supplied to satisfy the hungers of earth. A new day has truly dawned because Jesus has come. Man now has a way of escape and can have abiding hope.

(4) *New relationship to the Father set forth* (16:23–31).

—Jesus promised, "I leave the world, and go to the Father" (v. 28). This assurance helped change sorrow into joy. It assisted the followers of Jesus to comprehend that the grave was not an end. It gave opportunity for a glorious manifestation of limitless power.

Note Jesus' many statements of the intimacy of relationship between believers and the Father. Disciples are encouraged to ask the Father for what they need (vv. 23–26), to recognize that the Father loves them (v. 27). Knowing that Jesus was going to the Father would give the disciples an added feeling of closeness to God.

These facts call for the followers of Jesus to enter into their new, intimate relationship with a loving Heavenly Father. They are to turn from their loneliness and receive comfort, to turn from transgression and know forgiveness, to turn from strife and find peace.

(5) *Peace promised* (16:33).—Note that the comforting words of verse 33 follow the disturbing words of verse 32. Jesus was revealing to his disciples that he foreknew their failures. That very night they would "be scattered" when Jesus was arrested. But, in spite of their human weakness, he offered them his gift of peace.

"That in me ye might have peace" is a secret the world needs. It is a promise which the followers of Christ have never fully claimed for themselves or for any given generation. No wonder many wars have raged. Men have not believed what Jesus was saying to the extent of following it fully. Peace has been sought in the world in so many ways other than Jesus' way.

What is the secret of such peace? Hear the glorious assurance, "Be of good cheer; I have overcome the world." We may well rejoice that the Holy Spirit brought these words to John's mind, and led the apostle to include them in his witness to Jesus.

SUGGESTED ACTIVITIES FOR DEPTH STUDY

Some areas for Scripture searching, interpretation, and discussion are suggested:

1. What philosophy of life did Jesus state in his reply to the seeking Greeks (John 12:24–26)? How did this statement relate to the Greeks' question? Can one really "see" Jesus without accepting the death-life principle he stated? How did this incident help to prepare the disciples for the death of Jesus, with the events which accompanied it?

2. Wherein would the disciples be strengthened and encouraged, during the events leading to Jesus' arrest, by the realization that Jesus had foreknowledge of Judas' betrayal? Does it help us to know that, no matter what circumstances we get into, our Lord has not been taken by surprise?

3. As you read John 14, mark the statements that could have brought assurance to the disciples if they had recalled them in the dark days immediately following the crucifixion. Underline those statements that will help you to have faith and courage in dark days.

4. In John 16:1, 33 note Jesus' statements of the purpose which guided the discourse recorded in chapters 15–16. The author of this study book points out that Jesus prepared his disciples by assuring them they were a chosen people, a responsible people, and would be a people of strength and victory. Find verses that show Jesus told his disciples they would also be a hated people. Consider how each of these predictions or promises could help to prepare disciples in any age for meeting the tests that face them.

CHAPTER 9

9

Deity Revealed in Humiliation

John 13:1-20; 17-19

THIS STUDY HAS dealt almost exclusively with the incidents and teachings found only in the Gospel of John. No witness to Jesus, however, could be complete without regard for his death and resurrection, which are recorded in each of the Gospels.

In his record of the last week John bears witness to the God-man, superbly victorious. The blended humanity and deity of Jesus is apparent as we see him girding on a towel (13:1-19), interceding in the high-priestly prayer (chap. 17), yielding to human injustice (18:2 to 19:16), and drinking the cup of death (19:17-42).

I. GIRDING ON A TOWEL (13:1-20)

The things which transpired in the upper room on the night of Jesus' betrayal were tremendous in their meaning and impact for the disciples and for us. "When Jesus knew that his hour was come that he should depart out of this world unto the Father, having loved his own . . . he loved them unto the end."

1. The Holy Place

The public ministry was over. Private moments with the twelve were golden opportunities. Eating the Passover feast, they were also being prepared for the institution of the Lord's Supper. In the upper room Jesus demonstrated the depths to which love would carry the lover that the loved ones may be blessed. Words of comfort and farewell were in order.

The emotional impact of this last evening with the disciples gave them such hallowed memories that it was natural that they would return to this same place before Pentecost to await the coming of the Holy Spirit according to promise. We assume that it was in this room that the Holy Spirit came upon them and prepared them to launch their mission of world conquest in Jesus' name.

2. *Humility Demonstrated* (13:3–17)

Never was deity more beautifully demonstrated than when the towel-girded Jesus washed the disciples' feet. The divine One stooped low to meet human need. Nothing reveals the humility, the self-emptying, of Jesus more clearly than this action. Usually, learners knelt at the feet of their teacher and lord. But here Jesus reversed the tradition.

Jesus exalted himself when he humbled himself in order to honor his disciples. They never got away from this demonstration of Jesus' high concept of the work they were destined to do on earth as Christians and witnesses. Dust and mud, sandals and shoes, are lowly indeed. The task of washing feet usually fell to servants. Jesus revealed the importance of the spirit of service in the heart of the Christian, in which the welfare of others is to take precedence.

The spiritual significance of this incident is indicated in the conversation between Peter and Jesus (vv. 8–10). Williams records it:

Peter said to Him, "You must never wash my feet!"

Jesus answered, "Unless I do wash you, you can have no share with me."

Simon Peter said to Him, "Lord, do not stop with my feet, then; but wash my hands and face too!"

Jesus said to him, "Anyone who has just taken a bath has no need of washing anything but his feet, but he is clean all over."

Jesus' answer seems to say, in symbol, that Peter's heart was already cleansed through "the washing of regeneration" (Titus 3:5). However, Peter and all the disciples would need constant cleansing of their walk if they were to share with Christ in bringing an effective witness to the world. This truth of cleansing of a believer's daily walk John dealt with more fully in his first epistle (1 John 1:7). Because of its importance in the preparation of the men to whom Jesus would soon entrust the ministry of witnessing, the Master presented it dramatically as well as verbally.

3. *Disloyalty and Fidelity* (13:18-20)

We have already studied Jesus' dealing with Judas in the upper room, noting how he sought to prepare the other disciples for the shock of the betrayal. We look again at the scene, considering how the deity of Jesus shone through.

Men in the upper room saw two contrasting acts: Jesus washing the disciples' feet and his dismissal of Judas from their company as the betrayer. Already Jesus had alluded to the betrayal (6:70), although the other disciples apparently did not, at the time, know that Judas was meant. Prior to the dismissal of Judas, Jesus revealed that even the betrayal was included in prophecy about Messiah. He recalled Psalm 41:9: "Yea, mine own familiar friend, in whom I trusted, which did eat of my bread, hath lifted up his heel against me." How cruel and ugly disloyalty can become! Jesus' foreknowledge of the betrayal could not lessen its sting.

Jesus stated why he was forewarning his disciples: "That, when it is come to pass, ye may believe that *I am he*" [author's italics]. Thus, even the adverse situation would be a witness to the deity of Jesus. (Note the "I am" of v. 19.) Jesus refused to be embittered by the betrayal. Rather, he stressed the positive note and magnified the beauty of loyalty with the words, "He that receiveth me receiveth him that sent me."

II. INTERCEDING FOR HIS OWN (Chap. 17)

John's witness to Jesus given through the record of the high priestly prayer is unsurpassed. Had this record alone been preserved and all the rest of John's Gospel lost, it would seem that men still could have known that Jesus was God. In this memorable prayer Jesus embraced all believers through the centuries—even us—and demonstrated his compassionate concern for all mankind.

1. *Noble Example* (17:1)

Jesus was a man of prayer. Although most of his public prayers were brief, his private prayers sometimes lasted through the night. The New Testament records thirteen or more specific instances when Jesus prayed. John recorded three of the prayers (11:41–42; 12:27–28; 17). If any man questions the value of prayer, he should analyze the significant place of prayer in the ministry of Jesus.

2. *Redemptive Mission and Coming Glory* (17:2–8)

The prayer of Jesus recorded in John 17 is far more than an example. Throughout there is clearly expressed Jesus' awareness of responsibility as the Redeemer whom God had sent. His universal authority is clearly stated. He spoke of the glory he had with the Father before the world was and which he was to receive again (v. 5). Jesus, the divine Son, was talking with the Father on a basis transcending human understanding.

3. *Intercession for Christians* (17:9–23)

It is significant that Jesus' prayer here was for Christians. He wanted them to be good witnesses; he prayed for their understanding, strength, and endurance. He prayed more directly for believers than for sinners. Indeed, he said, "I pray not for the world." This did not mean he lacked interest in the lost world. He had come to die for the lost world. In line with that purpose, his prayer was for the Christians who would be going out into the world like sheep among wolves to win men. Through such witness would lost men be won.

Jesus refused to pray that his disciples be taken immediately out of the world (v. 15). From whom would Christian testimony come if the Christian witnesses were removed from the earth? As Matthew records, the followers of Jesus are to be salt to flavor. Like salt they are to halt the decay of a world rotting in decomposition caused by sin. They are to shine as lights in the world. Christians on earth are direly needed, and their testimony will be most effective. They must remain and witness faithfully.

Jesus, while he did not ask for organizational union, prayed for the spiritual unity of Christians of the present and the future (v. 22). Fellow believers are linked together by a common faith, a common heritage of Christian experience, and a common mission which is the redemption of lost men. Christ alone can bring spiritual unity among believers in him.

4. Burden for the World (17:23–26)

Again Jesus prayed for oneness and love among Christian believers. He prayed "that *they may be made perfect* [author's italics] in one" (v. 23), in order that the world may know that God had sent his Son.

Here, as all through the Gospel of John, there is the sustained emphasis that Jesus is divine. He alone can cement the hearts of men in mutual love. The true unity of Christians would declare his deity. In a divided, warring, disintegrating world, Jesus is to be the focal point, the unifying force. Through him, hearts are made tender and love heals wounds of division and brings about the common heartbeat of purpose that Christ shall be exalted. Jesus is the pivotal point around whom all of life revolves. Without him, one's life and even his world are sure to be shattered.

Confident that he had fully done the will of God, Jesus struck the note of victory even as he faced the cross: "I have declared unto them thy name, and will declare it: that the love wherewith thou hast loved me may be in them, and I in them" (v. 26). The world that had not known him was on his heart. How heavy the load! Such weight will drive a man of compassion to his knees in prayer.

III. YIELDING TO HUMAN INJUSTICE (18:1 to 19:16)

Following the high-priestly prayer, Jesus moved on to the garden of Gethsemane. John's record bears witness to the courage of Jesus and to his confidence that the cross was the way to achieve his purpose of world redemption.

1. *Betrayed, Arrested, Forsaken* (18:1–11)

If Jesus had any tendency to cowardice, he would have given way to it when the cohort of Roman soldiers, accompanied by some officers of the chief priests and Pharisees and led by Judas, came with blazing lamps and clanking weapons to capture him in the garden. Jesus faced them in boldness, asking, "Whom seek ye?" When they replied, "Jesus of Nazareth," he simply answered, "I am he." The attackers were disconcerted by the courage of Jesus and fell backward in awe.

So unjust was Judas' act of treachery and so one-sided was the display of force in capturing a peaceable, unarmed man, that Peter in his impulsiveness became dreadfully upset. Resorting to the human tendency to meet violence with violence, Peter drew a sword. With a mighty stroke he severed Malchus' ear. Evidently, Peter was swinging blindly with the intent to defend his Lord with his own life. Much had he yet to learn before he could bear true witness for the Saviour.

Jesus was calm. He never proved his greatness more than when under fire. Chiding Peter for such a spontaneous display of temper, Jesus cautioned him to put away the sword. From other accounts we learn that Jesus healed Malchus' ear.

He expressed willingness to face whatever was to come and to drink the cup of suffering and death willingly, regardless of bitterness. And how bitter it was, because it was the cup not alone of death, but of death for sin. Jesus would not take the easy way out.

2. *Failure of Man's Justice* (18:12–14, 19–24)

Annas was a former high priest who still had much influence. From him justice might have been expected. He was a man of maturity and experience. Certainly he should have been able to differentiate between guilt and innocence, being no novice in court trials. He was father-in-law to Caiaphas, the high priest. Thus, Annas could have had easy access to Caiaphas for consultation if needed. These were not men with mere civil authority, but men with ecclesiastical responsibilities. They were supposed to be masters of divine law as well as human law, and they should have been able to make interpretations accurately.

Jesus, being questioned, invited the calling of witnesses who had heard him speak (v. 21). He welcomed an honest and open examination of his words and deeds. Instead of granting his request and making an objective inquiry, an officer of the Sanhedrin standing nearby struck him a blow, reprimanding him for not falling into their trap baited with unfair questions. Jesus urged that they cite the wrong, if he had done wrong (v. 23). If he were right, how could the blow be justified? They demanded death, but could not even justify a brutal slap in the face.

Annas, seeing that something had to be done to absolve himself, bound Jesus and sent him to Caiaphas. Maybe a more youthful mind could devise plausible explanation that the public would accept as a reason for the arrest—an explanation which could at least border on justice. It seems that Annas and Caiaphas were both men with keen minds and weak knees. They had thought Jesus was on trial, but they found themselves condemned for their own failures as he stood before them. They were tried and condemned in their own court by their own acts.

3. *Failure of the Faithful* (18:15–18, 25–27)

The followers of Jesus were terrified at the situation. How could normally intelligent men act so much like beasts? To witness the brutal treatment of Jesus was a frightening experience. Peter could not take it. His faith did not fail or die (cf. Luke 22:32) but it did go into eclipse. His courage wavered, and he denied his Lord. The flesh is indeed weak, and pride is futile.

Although Peter had said earlier that he would die for Jesus, things did not look the same when he stared at the hostile faces of the officers of the Sanhedrin and servants of the high priest. He was accosted first by the servant of the high priest and then by a relative of Malchus, whose ear Peter had cut off. Each accused him of being a friend of Jesus. Those direct accusations triggered terror in Peter's heart and brought denial to his lips.

Having followed Jesus to the trial, because he could not agree for Jesus to face the accusers alone, Peter had found himself caught in an unexpected situation where he would either stand tall or fall flat. Maybe he had trusted too much in himself or in the sword and not enough in the Christ to give him needed courage. Still, Jesus knew what was in Peter's heart, for Jesus knew well how much faith and manliness were required to face such human injustice. It must not be overlooked that, of the other disciples, only John had even attempted to be as near as Peter was during the trial (v. 16).

Disappointed at his own weakness in a time of test, Peter went out and wept bitterly. His repentance was deep. No wonder Jesus forgave him and later sent him forth to his greatest service. Peter's remembrance of his miserable failure helped him to face future testings with humility and faith.

4. *Innocence Condemned* (18:28 to 19:16)

The Jewish court had no power to condemn a man to die by capital punishment. They could express opinions and wishes, but they could not execute their victims. It was necessary, therefore, that Jesus be tried before the Roman governor if the sentence of the Jewish tribunal was to be confirmed.

Pontius Pilate, the Roman judge, heard the case of Jesus. He acted in the weakest political fashion, yielding to human clamor. In doing so he murdered justice and law in public. He failed to act responsibly and decisively when necessary; he compromised his own convictions under stress. It is certain that he disobeyed his own conscience, for he had declared, "I find in him no fault at all" (18:38). Still, Pilate allowed Jesus to be killed. The crowds felt that Pilate should simply have condemned Jesus on the basis of the verdict of the Jewish court, accepting their accusation as tantamount to condemnation (18:30).

Pilate sought a private interview with Jesus and heard him with interest. Jesus asserted his kingship, but he stated that it was in the spiritual realm rather than the physical. Hearing Jesus tell of his mission of divine kingship, Pilate must have been either skeptical or curious. At least he turned immediately with the question, "What is truth?"

From a man who had been assigned the task of ferreting out truth in order to hand down a valid verdict, this question seems queer. Pilate either confessed his frustration or revealed his skepticism by trying to embarrass Jesus with troublesome questions, as others had done. At that point Pilate went again before the crowds to declare the innocence of Jesus. But his failure to set Jesus free reveals this Roman governor's fear of mobs.

In an effort to find a way out of his dilemma, Pilate sought to use an old Roman concession once made to Palestine. It provided that on the Passover authorities could set free any prisoner designated by the people. Pilate seemed sure that they would ask that Jesus be set free, since his innocence was apparent. The Roman ruler was shocked when the mobs clamored for Barabbas, the known criminal, to be released and for Jesus, the innocent, to be crucified. From that point on Pilate played their ugly game of injustice by their own self-written rules of hate.

To quell the mobs and appease them in their anger, Pilate had Jesus publicly scourged (19:1). The soldiers placed a mock crown of thorns and a purple robe upon him, ridiculing his claims of kingship. Men cried, "Crucify him," and the chief priest and the officers became the cheerleaders of the bloodthirsty crowd.

Jesus was held up in ridicule with the cries, "Behold your King!" (19:14). He was delivered up to be crucified in spite of innocence. Base and beastly men showed how low a depraved humanity will go to have its way. But the Saviour's finest hour came out of man's lowest deed. Their hate had given him opportunity to prove his love.

Few things are more surprising than the spirit of the Jewish crowds, voiced by their own leaders, "We have no king but Caesar" (19:15). And this was said after years of effort to cut off the yoke of Caesar in Palestine. By avowing their allegiance to Rome, they had compromised their own integrity in order to get Jesus out of their sight. The crowd before Pilate condemned Jesus, even as every sinner since Adam has done. They accomplished in fact what evil men through the centuries will never cease achieving in token until Jesus comes again.

IV. DRINKING THE CUP OF DEATH (19:17–42)

Each of the Gospels tells of the crucifixion. John emphasizes that he is giving testimony as an eyewitness (v. 35). He records only three sayings from the cross (vv. 26, 28, 30). He cites two references to the Old Testament (vv. 36–37). The first linked Jesus with the Passover lamb (Ex. 12:46). The other was a quotation recognized as messianic (Psalm 22: 16).

1. *Scorn and Love at Calvary* (19:17–27)

Golgotha—which we assume was a hill which bore the shape of a skull—was where Jesus was destined to die. The centurion supervising the gruesome task seemed experienced in his assignment. Pilate in derision had placed an inscription over Jesus' head, declaring in three languages that he was the king of the Jews. Citizens tried to get Pilate to remove the sign, but the governor stood firm. Refusing to compromise now would not cost him much, and to some extent might ease his conscience for the cowardice he had shown when he allowed Jesus to be condemned unjustly.

Gambling soldiers, according to custom, took the garments of Jesus to divide them. They cast lots over his tunic, as prophecy had declared (Psalm 22:18). Barclay comments that his tunic may have been the type worn by a high priest. Truly Jesus was that and more.

Courageously, the mother of Jesus risked her own life to come to the cross by the side of Jesus, along with John. In tender concern Jesus committed her care to John the apostle, his beloved friend. Jesus knew that John in his loving manner would care for her every physical need, but the heavy burden of her broken heart was one which John could not mend.

2. *The Cry of Thirst* (19:28–30)

The Synoptic Gospels tell of miraculous phenomena at the time of the crucifixion. John limits his discussion mostly to Jesus and what happened to him.

The error of gnosticism caused John to emphasize the fact that Jesus was God in the flesh, a truth many had difficulty accepting. It was John who recorded the cry, "I thirst," magnifying the human aspect of Jesus' nature. Those who heard his cry gave him vinegar—which was hardly more than a sour wine—placed to his lips by a hyssop reed. This use of the hyssop had meaning (Ex. 12:22), reminding the thoughtful observers of the Passover lamb and God's miraculous deliverance of his people from Egypt. When Jesus had received the vinegar, he "gave up his spirit" (v. 30, ASV). The act was voluntary. Earlier he had declared regarding his own life, "I have power to lay it down, and I have power to take it again" (10:18).

3. *Jesus Pronounced Dead* (19:31–37)

Under Jewish law it was necessary to remove the bodies from the crosses before sunset, since that hour marked the beginning of the sabbath (v. 31). How strange that men who grossly violated the commandment, "Thou shalt not kill," were so meticulous about obeying the law regarding the burial of the victims' bodies before dark. Even so, the Jews were more merciful than the Romans, who were never willing to speed the death of a victim by inflicting additional physical injuries, and who never bothered with burial after their victims had died.

Permission was received from Pilate for the legs of these victims to be broken to hasten death. But when the soldiers came to Jesus, they found him already dead. It took no permission, therefore, for them to pierce the side of his corpse. His legs were not broken. (Cf. Ex. 12:46; Psalm 34:20.) Hence, his death was in keeping with the offering of the paschal lamb—which truly Jesus was. The robbers on either side of him, however, were not spared the final crushing death blows.

4. *Burial of Jesus* (19:38–42)

Joseph of Arimathea and Nicodemus, who had not shown sufficient courage while Jesus lived, did do so now, after he had died. Nicodemus brought spices to use lavishly upon the body, and Joseph was anxious for his own tomb to be used to lay Jesus away.

Joseph and Nicodemus apparently were members of the Sanhedrin. Once Nicodemus had spoken in behalf of Jesus (John 7:50–52). But when Jesus was on trial before that group, not one of these friends dared to speak in his defense. How dreadful their silence must have seemed to Jesus. Jesus' death changed the two men from cowards to heroes. They took a bold step when they asked for Jesus' body to give it decent burial.

The new tomb was used, but the crucified Christ who was buried there had already made bold new men out of these believers. The question is natural: Can any believer behold Calvary in all of its meaning and yet be cowardly or silent?

SUGGESTED ACTIVITIES FOR DEPTH STUDY

Here are four portraits of Jesus' deity. Yet, at first glance they do not seem to be portrayals of deity. Form four study groups, each with a leader. Each group will take the Scripture passage cited for one of the four main divisions of the outline and examine it for actions or statements that do show Jesus as God the Son. Examine the facts that seem at variance with the idea of Jesus' deity. In the discussion that follows the reports consider (1) how the death-life principle stated by Jesus (John 12:24–26) was being demonstrated in the life of Jesus, and (2) wherein Calvary is one of the highest demonstrations of deity.

CHAPTER 10

10

Continuing Witness

John 20–21

THE MESSAGE THAT Jesus was alive again brought electric excitement to the followers who had felt abandoned since they had watched him die. They were surer than ever that God was real and alive. The Master had not failed them. They would be winners in the name and the strength of the victorious Christ.

John records certain encounters which believers had with the risen Christ. Each of these encounters made of the believer a witness for Christ.

I. THE WITNESS OF THE EMPTY TOMB (20:1–10)

John gives emphasis to the visit of Mary Magdalene to the tomb. The Synoptic Gospels mention other women as well. (Cf. Matt. 28:1; Mark 16:1; Luke 23:55 to 24:1.)

1. Early Morning Visit (20:1a)

It is not surprising that Mary Magdalene would come to the tomb at such an early hour. Jesus had done so much for her that she could never repay or forget. Luke reports that Jesus had cast seven devils from her. She could never adequately show the true gratitude her heart felt for the change Jesus brought to her life.

2. Amazing Discovery (20:1–2)

A large circular stone slab was set in a groove next to the wall of the tomb. This stone could be rolled before the door opening in such a way that its weight kept it in place. Mary was surprised to notice, in the darkness of the early morning, that the stone had been rolled back. Her first impression was that the same mob which had been so brutal in their crucifixion had wanted to heap their hatreds on Jesus' dead body in ghoulish fashion.

Mary knew instinctively that this was not the sort of situation for women to handle, so she rushed to find Peter and John—who humbly refers to himself as "the other disciple, whom Jesus loved." Not being able to understand it all did not reduce Mary's love or her expressions of personal commitment.

Mary's going to Peter showed that she had confidence in him. Did she know of his denial of his Lord? To Mary, Peter was still the leader of the disciples. If she knew of his temporary failure, she must have known also of his sorrow and repentance. To her that was sufficient.

3. The Truth Comprehended (20:3-9)

Peter, accompanied by John, ran excitedly to confirm Mary's report. John, apparently the younger, arrived first. He paused at the door of the tomb, either in exhaustion or puzzlement as to the meaning of all this. When Peter arrived, he rushed headlong into the tomb. Then John stepped to his side. Together they assessed the situation. It became immediately obvious that Jesus' body had not been stolen away, as Mary had feared. The graveclothes gave no evidence of foul play.

John, the disciple of love, "saw, and believed" (v. 8). Love always seems to be the first to understand.

So much of significance that Jesus had said lacked full meaning for the disciples until they saw the empty tomb. Their experiences had been too limited, their faith too small, and their love too cold. Is not that the experience of most of us in life's crises?

II. Mary Becomes a Witness (20:10–18)

The disciples, after observing the empty tomb, turned away in amazement to their own homes. It was too much for them, it seemed, to fully comprehend what had occurred.

1. Special Appearance to Mary (20:11–14)

Upon the departure of the disciples, Mary, standing outside the tomb, stopped to look inside. What she saw was both perplexing and glorious. Two angels were clearly visible, robed in brilliant white. One had seated himself where the head of Jesus had lain; the other, where his feet had been.

The angels asked Mary about her weeping. Straightforwardly she replied that it was because she could not find the body of her Lord. Turning at that moment, she saw Jesus, but tears seem to have blinded her eyes to his identity. Despair momentarily concealed from her the fact of victory. Though love had revealed much, she had not understood all. She stood perplexed.

2. Probing Questions and Willing Witness (20:15–16)

Coming to Mary, Jesus asked whom she was seeking. Still blinded by despair, Mary thought him to be the gardener. She begged that, if he had carried the body away, he would be kind enough to tell where it had been placed so she might take it and bury it decently.

Only when Jesus called, "Mary," and she heard her name did the fact possess her that she was in the presence of her living Lord. Overwhelmed with emotion, she cried in the Aramaic dialect, "Rabboni" (teacher).

Love, built on personal faith, seems to reveal more about Jesus than anything else. Mary and John, two who were noted for their lavish devotion, were among the first to grasp the fact of the resurrection, even though at the moment they were still unable to understand the impact of it.

3. *Sharing the Message of Victory* (20:17-18)

Mary was so overjoyed that she wanted to cling to Jesus lest he disappear again. It was as if she needed the grasp of her human hands to keep him nearby. Jesus admonished, "Stop clinging to Me" (v. 17, NASB). Mary found herself wanting to hold to this overflowing feeling of victory. Her feeling was akin to that of the disciples who wanted to linger on the mount of transfiguration.

Such possessive love may be thrilling to the soul of the Christian, but it has in it an element of selfishness. Although Jesus is Lord, he is not so much to be possessed as he is to be shared. Sharing him holds him more closely than trying to cling to him. Jesus' command to Mary was that she go and tell the truth of the resurrection to his followers.

With the ascension near at hand, Jesus wanted every possible moment to prepare his followers for their continued devoted discipleship. Hence, Mary was commanded to go to them and give his message: "I ascend unto my Father, and your Father; and to my God, and your God." She is the first recorded witness to bear the words of the risen Christ.

III. THE DISCIPLES COMMISSIONED TO WITNESS (20:19-31)

Because of their fear of the angry Jews, who had already proved that they would show no mercy, the disciples met in the upper room. It was a spot of glorious happenings and became a place of hallowed memories.

1. *First Appearance to the Group* (20:19-20)

These disciples needed every help they could get to face and overcome their fears. They might well be the next victims of death at the hands of the same unjust mobs who had clamored for Jesus' crucifixion. Gathered behind locked doors, they feared the worst. Imagine their sudden elation when Jesus appeared inside the room without so much as a knock, greeting them with the traditional, "Peace be unto you." Knowing their need for assurance, he showed them his hands and his side. Terror was instantly replaced with rejoicing. Defeat was overcome by the sense of sure victory.

2. Commission and Empowering (20:21–23)

Jesus felt that the disciples needed challenge as well as comfort. Thus he said, "As my Father hath sent me, even so send I you" (v. 21). Knowing they could not go forth alone, he declared that the Holy Spirit would be within them to provide courage for the conquest.

The whole world was thus laid on their shoulders. Their ministry was God's plan for worldwide missionary activity. If the disciples failed, the whole earth would suffer (v. 23).

Although churches cannot forgive sins, they are entrusted with the proclamation of the message of redemption. God has no other messengers for his truth than Christians.

3. Thomas Absent (20:24–25)

Thomas was not present with the other disciples during these glorious moments. The disciples who heard Jesus had difficulty communicating what they had seen and heard, and the magnificent meaning of their experience. Thomas indicated a desire for an experience which would give him evidence beyond any dispute that Jesus was indeed risen. He tended to doubt that which someone else had experienced and was telling him. Although Thomas is called the doubter, it must be noted that he had an open mind. He also had a desire to confirm the truth.

4. Thomas Present (20:26–29)

The following week the disciples were again gathered, and this time Thomas was present. Again Jesus appeared suddenly, and addressed himself to the needs of Thomas: "Touch my hands; feel my side; believe!" No touch was needed to convince Thomas. His response, "*My* Lord and *my* God [author's italics]," showed Thomas' belief that Jesus was alive. The witness of Thomas proclaimed the disciple's assurance that Jesus belonged to him and he belonged to Jesus. This confession linked Thomas with Christ in closest union. He was not simply Lord, he was Thomas' own Lord. Thomas had demanded evidence, and Jesus met the challenge completely.

Jesus felt constrained to chide Thomas by complimenting the faith of Christians who would never have such opportunities of physical evidence, but who, nevertheless, would believe and join the company of witnesses.

We must admire Thomas for his honesty. He would not claim that he believed so long as there were lingering doubts. When he saw the evidences given, there was no more hesitating. His commitment was complete, for Jesus was then declared as his Lord. Thomas went further than many men who, although they have yearned to have Jesus as Saviour, have never wanted him to be their Lord, lest they might have to go somewhere against their wills or to speak a word which might cost them something.

5. *Other Manifestations* (20:30–31)

John the evangelist readily declares his inability to tell everything about Jesus. All truth cannot be concealed in the confines of any book. Many other "signs" were performed before the disciples, which were too numerous to record (v. 30). Yet the influence of Jesus' words and deeds was felt and remembered by the disciples.

At this point John gives the key to all the witness set forth in his Gospel. "These [things] are written, that ye might believe that Jesus is the Christ, the Son of God; and that believing ye might have life through his name" (v. 31). The objective was faith for those who sought answers to life's baffling problems, but who could never observe with their own eyes the miracles Jesus did nor like Thomas be invited to confirm the facts by the touch of their own hands.

The apostle had not set out to write a full biography of Jesus, but to bear witness to his mission and ministry on earth. The millions who have read John's Gospel through the past nineteen hundred years have testified that he did accomplish well what he set out to do.

It must not be overlooked that the Gospel of John is addressed largely to Christians, so that in their witnessing they may know what to say and that in saying there will be no room for doubt. Men are to believe not just for the sake of believing; they are to believe that they may live and share. To do so is life abundant.

IV. FORWARD IN CONQUEST (Chap. 21)

As John's Gospel has a prologue, so there is an epilogue. Both are appropriate and timely. The prologue begins by declaring that Jesus is God and setting forth the nature and the purpose of Jesus on earth. The epilogue answers, What next? Where is this revelation to lead us? What does it produce in our lives? How are we, as God's children, to be involved in his work? The prologue lays the foundation. The epilogue is the green light, the signal of advance.

1. *Attracting Attention* (21:1–8)

To bide their time until the appropriate moment, some of the disciples returned to their former profession of fishing. The night brought hard work without accomplishment, even though night is usually the best time for catching fish.

At daybreak a voice called to ask if they had secured any food to eat. The response was in the negative. Their failure was evidenced by completely empty nets. Jesus ordered from the shore that they cast the nets on the other side of the boat. When they obeyed, their nets were filled, and the men had difficulty landing the huge catch—one hundred fifty-three fish.

"That disciple whom Jesus loved" (John himself) recognized the speaker on land and cried out to Peter that it was the Lord. Putting on his outer garment (fishermen wore only loin cloths when they worked) Peter hurled himself into the water to swim to Jesus. Other disciples came ashore and the fellowship was a refreshing one in the dawn of a new day.

2. *Meeting Human Needs* (21:9–14)

Upon landing, the disciples found a charcoal fire, with cooking food and bread. Peter was instructed to supply some of the fishes just caught.

Again Jesus assumed the role of servant. Taking bread, he gave it to the disciples. Earlier he had washed their feet. Now he served them food. So clearly did he indicate his spirit and character that there was no doubting now as to who he was. He was manifested to his disciples. They had no lingering questions about the reality or about the glory of his resurrection. Jesus, the risen Christ, was alive before them.

Appearing with nail prints and pierced side, his body continued to have features like his earthly form, but it was a glorified body, no longer bound by space or confined by locked doors.

The risen Christ had a real body. That no one could deny. His appearance could not have been a hallucination. No apparition could have fed the disciples as he did. It was Jesus himself now alive, and no more need there be timidity in saying so. This fact could be declared with boldness and conviction.

3. *Sending Disciples to Serve* (21:15–25)

The table talk at breakfast time by the seashore answered many questions the disciples must have been asking. Where were they to start their ministry? How were they to begin?

Jesus gave the cue. They were to start where they were with what they had and were to do whatever they could with divine help.

Peter continued to be the recognized leader of the disciples. As he went, so would the others go. So Jesus began by addressing him, "Peter, lovest thou me more than these?" These what? Likely Jesus gestured to the boat, the net, the paddles, the sails, and all the rigging of the fisherman. Was it not Peter who had said earlier, "I go a fishing" (v. 3), and led the other disciples back to their nets? Now he was called by Christ to give these up. Dear though they might be in memory to him, Jesus was to be loved more. Anything and everything must be laid aside that Jesus' work might be carried on.

The English language fails us here as we try to grasp significant shades of Bible meaning in these next few verses. Clear distinctions are given in the Greek that the English language has difficulty conveying.

Two of the words in the Greek language which are translated "love" in our English New Testament are meaningfully used. One is *phileo,* which carries the idea of brotherhood, implying fondness or fellowship. It is of the same root as the word used in the name Philadelphia, "city of brotherly love." The other word is *agapao,* which is the word used of divine love in John 3:16. Usually *agapao* refers to a higher, more spiritual love, while *phileo* indicates a human liking or affection, not quite so noble or high, but still a noble emotion. The conversation between Jesus and Peter plays dramatically on the meaning of these two words.

Jesus began the play on words by asking, "Simon, son of Jonas, lovest [*agapao*] thou me more than these?" (v. 15). Peter replied, "Yea, Lord; thou knowest that I love [*phileo*] thee." Jesus had asked about divine love; Peter responded by declaring human affection for him.

How different this attitude was from the egotistical pride Peter had shown earlier, when he had said that all others might deny the Lord, but that he himself would be true to the end. Experience and failure at the trial of Jesus had taken away his egotism and sense of self-sufficiency. His first response to Jesus' question showed a spirit of humility.

A second time Jesus asked the question, using *agapao* and referring to the divine love (v. 16). Again Peter replied with the lesser word, *phileo*, and gave assurance once more of his human affection.

The third time Jesus asked the question he dropped to the lower word and used *phileo* (v. 17), probing Peter, "Do you really have affection for me?" Feeling that Jesus was pressing him, Peter was grieved as he replied, again in the word for love which was in a lower case, "Thou knowest all things; thou knowest that I love [*phileo*] thee" (v. 17).

Experience had slain personal pride. Peter did not want to get himself out on a limb by claiming divine qualities and attributes, and then suffer subsequent humiliations again because he had depended too much on himself.

With Peter's repeated assurances of affection, Jesus replied "Feed my lambs" (v. 15). "Tend my sheep" (v. 16, ASV). "Feed my sheep" (v. 17). The statements gave the great commission in personal fashion. As love brought Jesus to earth, it must also carry believers forth into all the earth. Love compels. The disciple was called upon to feed and to share with the lambs, to tend and to shepherd the sheep. What a humble but impressive way to begin conquering a world! Yet this mission reveals the gist and essence of the gospel. Here is where the believer is to begin. Service is to be the true test of love, the best demonstration of faith. In the simplest deeds of service, Christian influence is to expand until the whole earth has heard and heeded.

Jesus, by predicting martyrdom for Peter, reminded him of the cost of discipleship and then urged him once more, "Follow me." There was much more meaning to this commandment now than when Peter and the others were called to discipleship, some three years before on the shores of Galilee. Peter did not have John's capacity for deep meditation nor Paul's ability for theological reasoning. But Peter would be capable of magnificent things because of the extent of his love, the depth of his devotion, and the measure of his dependence upon God.

Thus, John's Gospel has summarized and interpreted the life and the teachings of Jesus. If everything were given in detail, the libraries of earth would overflow in interpretation of the events. Space would not allow all to be said, but John gives enough.

Although John declares his writings fragmentary, they are so complete they would suffice to witness to Jesus, even if they were the only ones on earth. Through John's witness men can have clear evidence of why Jesus came, what he came to do, and what he did for the salvation of men. Reading John's Gospel, they know how Jesus reveals God and how he transforms human beings.

That which believers have heard and experienced of Christ they are now obligated to proclaim. What they know they are to tell. What they have learned they are to teach. Believers have been found that they might find; they have been won that they might win. This is the work of Christians until Jesus comes again.

SUGGESTED ACTIVITIES FOR ENRICHMENT

Effective role playing will enhance the awareness of reality in the scenes recorded in John 20–21. Let four class members, who have been asked previously to prepare, form a role playing panel. Include Mary, John, Thomas, and Peter. Each will tell, in first person singular, the experience recorded. Each should present his role in a spirit of triumph and conquest.

Suggestions for the Teacher

PURPOSE: The title and the author's statement in the introduction show the purpose of this study course book. Think how it relates to needs of your class members. You will seek to lead the learners *to examine the witness which John bears to Jesus in a way that will lead them to experience a fresh encounter with Jesus and a new determination to make him known to others.*

GENERAL SUGGESTIONS

Emphasize study of the biblical text. Learners cannot get the message of the study course book apart from use of the Bible passages. Encourage study of each chapter before the class period in which it will be discussed.

No doubt much of your procedure will involve displaying the appropriate chapter outline and using it to guide Scripture searching, to reinforce your lecture, to suggest questions for discussion, and/or to aid in summarizing. The generous use of references makes these outlines effective study guides.

Vary your procedures. Give emphasis to guided Scripture searching, but employ many techniques: reports, role playing, listening teams, research teams, concert reading, and—at proper times—lecture.

Note the proposals for depth-study activities found at the end of each chapter. Select for use in class some which seem within the interests and abilities of the class and within limits set by your time schedule and the size of your class. Encourage members to carry through as many of these activities as they will, in individual study. Be sure they distinguish between these suggestions for extra enrichment study and the questions mentioned in the requirements for credit (pp. ix–x).

If possible, make available to each class member a small, paperbound Gospel of John to use in marking. Gospels published by the American Bible Society are available at the Baptist Book Stores for a few cents each. Encourage systematic marking as the Gospel is read. For example, statements which show the deity of Jesus may be marked with blue. Those that refer to salvation or the atonement may be marked with red. Each occurrence of any form of the words "believe," "belief," or "faith" may be marked in a specific way.

The following suggestions are based on a five-night schedule with ten class periods, forty-five minutes or more in length.

FOREWORD AND CHAPTER 1

Comment about the eagerness with which a lover drinks up information about the beloved. State that each of us has the privilege of studying a message about his dearest friend, whose love is beyond measure. It was written by a man who knew this friend long before we did and who can, therefore, add to our understanding and appreciation of the Lord Jesus Christ. Be sure the purpose of this study, as stated in the Foreword, is clear.

Using a harmony of the Gospels, point to the blocks of copy found only in John's Gospel. Then show the large amount of copy found in one or more of the Synoptic Gospels but not in the Fourth Gospel.

Have the class find in John 20:31 the purpose which guided John. Suggest that each member underline this verse and use it as a guidepost to understanding why John selected the events and discourses which he included in his witness.

MINIPORTS: State that chapter 1 presents an overview of John's Gospel and its general relationship to the author's purpose. Display the outline for chapter 1. Form seven research teams. Try to have on each team at least one person who has read chapter 1. Each team will explore the material in the study course book related to one of the seven points under the first main topic in the outline. After four to six minutes call for the miniports (one-minute reports). As each report is made, record a brief summary of the main idea brought out.

GUIDED SCRIPTURE SEARCHING: Ask members to follow the second part of the chapter outline as a guide to finding and stating five significant truths about Christ which are brought out in John 1:1–5, 9–14.

FOLLOW-UP: Call attention to the suggestions for depth-study activities. Encourage each class member to follow suggestions 2, 3, and 4, as he continues his study. If resource materials are available, ask for volunteers to carry out the committee activities suggested in 4 and 5—if you will use their research later in the course. (See procedures suggested for chapters 3, 6.)

CHAPTER 2

State that John, the Gospel writer, used the testimony of others who knew Jesus to carry out the purpose stated in 20:31.

Display the chapter outline and note the three sources cited. (John the Baptist is named twice.) Propose that we see what witness to Jesus each of these could give, based on his own first-hand experience with the Christ.

GUIDED LISTENING BY ENTIRE CLASS: Call attention to the eight characterizations of Jesus listed under the first main topic of the outline. Ask class members to seek to discover these characterizations as the designated Scripture passages are read aloud by a well-prepared reader. After the reading, use questions as they may be needed to lead to statements validating the characterizations mentioned in the outline and to discussion of their significance.

LISTENING TEAMS: For the consideration of the second part of the outline, form five listening teams. As verses 35–51 are read from a favorite translation, each team will concentrate on one point in the outline. After the reading, have the experiences of the first disciples related by representatives from the teams, speaking in relay.

ROLE PLAYING: To present the third part of the outline, have a member, to whom previous assignment has been made, assume the role of John the Baptist. Using John 3:22–36 as a basis, he will soliloquize on his evaluation of Jesus some months after the Lord's baptism. If role playing is an unfamiliar procedure to your class members, you may wish to illustrate it by, yourself, stepping to one side and beginning: "I, John the Baptist, have observed Jesus during the months which have elapsed since I baptized him. I am convinced that . . ."

LISTENING AND DISCUSSION: Call attention to outline point IV and have John 10:40–42 read. Ask: What is the significance of the evaluation of the group mentioned here?

STIMULATING HOME STUDY, (chapters 3–4): If you plan to follow the suggestions offered for committee reports and research teams, be sure to make the needed assignments.

CHAPTER 3

Since the three events discussed are relatively familiar, they can probably be recalled in a brief time in answer to well-worded questions. Then, with your guidance, the class may follow the directions for the first depth-study activity suggested at the end of the chapter.

If a committee is ready, have a report on soul-winning verses in John's Gospel. If there is no committee report, decide how you will use activity 2.

CHAPTER 4

Comment that John records only seven miracles, aside from the resurrection of Jesus, and that five of these are found only in the Fourth Gospel. Raise the problem of why John selected these particular miracles.

RESEARCH TEAMS: Have John 20:31 quoted or read in unison by the entire class. Call attention to the chart at the end of chapter 4. By assignment made previously, designate seven research teams, each of which will consider one of the miracles named and report orally on what might be written in the appropriate point on the chart. Allow 3-5 minutes for teams to recall results of their home study and prepare to report. Encourage the class to decide if additions or revisions are needed in the information reported.

STIMULATING HOME STUDY (chapters 5–6): Note the suggestions for using nine study teams in a depth-study activity based on chapter 5. If the class accepts the idea, form the teams and let them make preparation before the chapter is studied in class. Encourage individual pursuit of suggestion 2. Call attention to the title of chapter 6. Look at the suggestions for depth-study activities given at the end of the chapter. Ask each class member to prepare to participate in the activities suggested.

CHAPTER 5

State that we have examined the witness to Jesus which came from the Forerunner, from hearers, from disciples, and from Jesus' miracles. In this chapter we gather together significant claims in which Jesus bore witness to his own nature.

REPORTS FROM STUDY TEAMS: If the nine study teams were set up prior to this class period, follow the first activity suggested at the end of chapter 5. After the reports, use questions to bring out the comprehensiveness of Jesus' ministry to each of us as it is revealed in the figures of speech used.

CHAPTER 6

Make reference to the frustration we feel when faced with destructive, false criticism. Suggest that a study of the experiences of Jesus in this area should help us to see how such criticism can be met in a constructive way.

RESEARCH AND REPORTS: The suggestion for depth study given at the end of the chapter are addressed to the class members. They will prove effective directions for you to use in guiding group learning activities in the class.

STIMULATING HOME STUDY (chapters 7–8): If a committee is to report on the feasts mentioned in John's Gospel, call attention to the fourth suggestion at the end of chapter 7. Encourage each class member to select and follow one or more of the suggestions for depth study as an individual activity.

Request members to examine the suggestions at the end of chapter 8, with a view to following them in class.

CHAPTER 7

Lead into a conversation about the pain which may be caused by lack of confidence on the part of one's own family and by criticism from those from whom one would have a right to expect support. Comment that Jesus experienced such pain in a deeper way than any of us have known, and that we shall deal with the way he met such opposition.

SCRIPTURE SEARCHING: Lead the class to use topics I, II, III, of the chapter outline as a guide to points to bring out through Scripture searching and comment. Encourage members who have done any of the suggested depth-study activities to enrich the discussion by sharing their findings. Suggestion 2 will be valuable as a group activity.

GUIDED LISTENING: As topic IV is considered, have read aloud the first Scripture passage indicated, while class listens to test the appropriateness of the author's first point. Encourage comments. Continue in a similar manner with each of the four points in the outline.

LECTURE AND REPORTS: Summarize the information presented under V. If a committee has been doing research on the feasts mentioned by John, let them report.

CHAPTER 8

Comment that after perhaps three years of training his disciples, Jesus was approaching his death. Within about two months they would be left to carry on his work. How could he prepare them? Our study involves passages from John 12–16.

GUIDED LISTENING AND RESPONSE: Ask class members to use the chapter outline to guide their listening as John 12:20–50 is read. Base discussion on the first activity suggested at the end of chapter 8. Continue in the same manner with the passages covered by outline topics II and III and depth-study suggestions 2 and 3.

As the class follows topic IV of the outline, give a résumé of the author's discussion of points 1, 2, 3. Have someone read statements from chapter 16 which assure Christ's followers of strength and victory.

STIMULATING HOME STUDY (chapters 9–10): Refer to depth-study suggestions at the end of chapter 9. Plan with the class for the four teams suggested, asking them to report at the next period. Arrange with four members to present the roles suggested at the end of chapter 10.

CHAPTERS 9–10

Base your procedures on the suggested activities at the close of each chapter. Be sure to end on a note of challenge and assurance.

SUGGESTED AUDIO-VISUAL MATERIALS

The filmstrip *John's Portrait of Jesus* (50 frames, color, recording) has been prepared specifically for use in connection with the study of JOHN'S WITNESS TO JESUS. It will be effective to show this filmstrip at some time prior to the first class period. It will also prove effective as a summary of the entire study.

Other projected aids will prove valuable as extracurricular materials. Selected frames may be used as interest centers. (See suggestions in the *Teaching Guide for John's Witness to Jesus* by Proctor, which is available from your Baptist Book Store.) Consult a current copy for your *Baptist Book Store Catalog* for descriptions and prices.

Chapter 2

FILMSTRIPS: *The Ministry of John the Baptist,* 30 frames; *The First Disciples,* 25 frames

MOTION PICTURE: *Message of John the Baptist,* 20 minutes

Chapter 3

MOTION PICTURES: *Nicodemus,* 20 minutes; *Woman at the Well,* 15 minutes

Chapter 4

> FILMSTRIP: *The Raising of Lazarus,* 40 frames
> MOTION PICTURES: *Jesus Heals the Man Born Blind,* 20 minutes; *The Raising of Lazarus,* 13 minutes

Chapter 7

> FILMSTRIPS: *Jesus, the Good Shepherd,* 22 frames; *Shepherd Life in Palestine,* 50 frames
> MOTION PICTURES: *Before Abraham Was, I Am,* 20 minutes; *I Am the Resurrection,* 20 minutes

Chapter 8

> FILMSTRIP: *The Last Supper,* 28 frames
> MOTION PICTURE: *The Upper Room,* 15 minutes

Chapter 9

> FILMSTRIP: *The Crucifixion,* 27 frames
> MOTION PICTURES: *Betrayal in Gethsemane,* 15 minutes; *Trial Before Pilate,* 15 minutes; *The Crucifixion,* 20 minutes

Chapter 10

> FILMSTRIPS: *John's Portrait of Jesus,* 50 frames, color, recording; *Jesus' Resurrection,* 21 frames; *Jesus' Later Appearances,* 21 frames
> MOTION PICTURE: *The Lord Is Risen,* 15 minutes

BIBLIOGRAPHY

The following books will prove stimulating in connection with this study. The listing of a book does not necessarily imply full agreement with everything in its contents.

BARCLAY, WILLIAM. *The Gospel of John,* 2 Vols.
CARTER, JOHN F. *A Layman's Harmony of the Gospels.*
CONNER, WALTER THOMAS. *The Epistles of John.*
DANA, HARVEY E. *Heavenly Guest: An Expository Analysis of the Gospel of John.*
EDERSHEIM, ALFRED. *Jesus the Messiah.*
ERDMAN, CHARLES. *The Gospel of John.*
FILSON, FLOYD V. *The Gospel According to John.*

HARRISON, EVERETT F. *The Son of God Among the Sons of Men*, o.p.

HULL, WILLIAM E. *The Gospel of John.*

LENSKI, RICHARD C. H. *The Interpretation of St. John's Gospel.*

MEYER, FREDERICK B. *Love to the Uttermost*, o.p.

—— *The Life and Light of Men, Volume II*, o.p.

—— *Gospel of John.*

MORGAN, G. CAMPBELL. *Gospel According to John.*

QUIMBY, CHESTER WARREN. *John the Universal Gospel*, o.p.

ROBERTSON, A. T. *A Harmony of the Gospels.*

—— *Epochs in the Life of the Apostle John*, o.p.

SMITH, T. C. *Jesus in the Gospel of John.*

SPEER, ROBERT E. *John's Gospel, The Greatest Book in the World*, o.p.

STIRLING, JOHN. *Atlas of the Life of Christ.*

TASKER, RANDOLPH V. G. *Commentary on the Gospel According to St. John.*

TENNEY, MERRILL C. *John: The Gospel of Belief.*

TURNER, GEORGE A. and MANTLEY, JULIUS R. *The Gospel According to John.*

YATES, KYLE M. *Preaching from John's Gospel.*

For Review and Written Work

1. After you read the Foreword, write a statement to show how the title of this book is in accord with the author's aim.

CHAPTER 1

2. What was John's stated purpose in writing his Gospel?

3. What distinctive feature of John's Gospel is emphasized in this chapter? Why could John be an effective witness to Jesus?

4. Since there is no statement in the Fourth Gospel that John wrote it, why do we feel sure he is the author?

5. Give at least one way in which the deity of Jesus is set forth in the prologue of John's Gospel.

CHAPTER 2

6. State eight claims about Jesus that can be found in the account which John, the Gospel writer, gives of the ministry of the Forerunner.

7. As the author of this study book discusses the experiences of the early disciples, he brings out five blessings Jesus gave to these earnest seekers. List these blessings.

8. What special significance does the continued witness of John the Baptist, as recorded in John 3:22-36, have?

CHAPTER 3

9. What is the central truth that Jesus presented to Nicodemus in the interview recorded in John 3?

10. How did Jesus relate his approach to the woman of Samaria to her felt need?

11. What do you consider to be the central teaching about Jesus in the account of the woman taken in adultery?

CHAPTER 4

12. What aspects of Jesus' nature are most clearly revealed in the account of the first miracle at Cana?

13. Name three miracles of healing recorded by John. Show the progression in the length of the affliction and, thus, in the degree of hopelessness in the three cases.

14. What truths about Jesus does John bring out in his record of the feeding of the five thousand?

15. Wherein did the raising of Lazarus transcend even Jesus' other miracles of raising the dead? What significant step did the opposition to Jesus take as a result of this miracle?

CHAPTER 5

16. Recall John's purpose in writing his Gospel. State briefly how the record of the nine "I am's" of Jesus discussed in this chapter accords with this purpose.

17. State at least four of the "I am's" of Jesus which show his ministry in behalf of the believer. Tell, in your own words, at least one blessing which is implied in each figure of speech you have cited.

18. State two "I am's" which involve Jesus' claim to deity.

CHAPTER 6

Complete the following statements to show the main teaching in each situation named:

19. Jesus used the occasion of cleansing the Temple as an opportunity to teach that – – – –

20. He used the problem situation that developed because of the healing of the man at Bethzatha to teach that – – – –

21. He used the misunderstanding of the multitudes following the feeding of the five thousand to teach that – – – –

CHAPTER 7

22. From your reading of the Scripture passages discussed in this chapter, what two accusations would you say were the focal points of the open opposition which the religious leaders launched against Jesus?

23. What actual character defamations were made against him?

24. To what physical danger was Jesus exposed in the various encounters with the religious leaders? What reason does John give to explain why Jesus was not arrested or stoned to death prior to the time of the crucifixion?

CHAPTER 8

25. Why was Jesus at pains to forewarn and strengthen his disciples?

26. What was the significance of Jesus' answer to the request of the Greeks, "We would see Jesus"?

27. Cite at least six reassuring truths Jesus taught during the discourse which is recorded in John 14–16.

28. What source of strength and wisdom in witnessing was assured to the disciples after Jesus left them?

CHAPTER 9

29. What aspects of Jesus' nature does John highlight in his account of Jesus' washing the disciples' feet?

30. Why did Jesus, in his prayer recorded in John 17, pray for believers rather than praying for the world?

31. Give at least two examples of how Jesus' deity was evident during his trials and crucifixion.

32. What proof can you offer that Jesus, by his death, made a new man of Nicodemus?

CHAPTER 10

33. Recall the different believers that John mentions by name in chapters 20–21. By various experiences they were prepared to be witnesses. However, there is a common element, essential to the experience of each one, which was needed to produce effective witnesses. Can you state what it was? Can anyone witness to something unless he has experienced it?

34. What do Jesus' words to the disciples in the upper room (John 20:21–23) reveal about (1) the nature of the ministry committed to them, and (2) the power for their task?

35. How was the commission to Peter stated in the epilogue to John's Gospel? Do you agree that other believers, even ourselves, are included in this commission?